Abandoned

I would like to dedicate this book to my four precious children. Without them I don't know how I would have got through this journey.

Monica

A TRUE STORY BY
MONICA ALLAN

With *SUNDAY TIMES BESTSELLING AUTHORS*
ANN AND JOE CUSACK

MIRROR BOOKS

MIRROR BOOKS

All of the events in this story are true,
but some names and details have been changed to
protect the identities of individuals.

© Monica Allan

1

Published in Great Britain and Ireland in 2023 by
Mirror Books, a Reach PLC business.

www.mirrorbooks.co.uk
@TheMirrorBooks

Print ISBN 9781915306326
eBook ISBN 9781915306333

Cover Design: Rick Cooke
Typesetting: Christine Costello

Printed and bound in Great Britain by
CPI Group (UK) Ltd, Croydon, CR0 4YY

Contents

PART THREE: WISHAW GENERAL HOSPITAL

PART FOUR: THE SUPREME COURT

Prologue

There was a familiar, fuggy smell in the changing rooms and the air itself was heavy with moisture. I tried to breathe in, but my lungs felt solid; filled with a setting cement. We found a place on the crowded plastic benches, and I unzipped the bag with trembling hands. The inside of my head was blank and empty, wiped clean by fear. But all around was bustle and chaos; children clamouring to get into their shorts and bathing costumes and off, into the pool. They couldn't wait to jump into the water. I couldn't wait to get away from it.

She took my hand firmly, my small fingers crushed by hers, and steered me out of the room and up the stairs.

There was a growing dread, a throbbing in my chest, but I tried to push it away and focus instead on inflating my daughter's armbands and adjusting her goggles. But it crept back in like a swirling fog, settling on me like a damp cloak.

Each step, each stair, felt further and further away from safety. Her hand tightened around mine and my frightened little heart clattered against my ribs. What now?

"Mummy, where's my towel? Have you brought the stripey one, the one I like?" The voice that relied on me was the one that snapped me back to the changing rooms and I formed a weak smile.

"I have it," I nodded.

Into the bathroom and with a practised flick of her wrist, she switched on the bath tap, full flow, the water gushing out like a burst dam.

"Come on," she urged, taking my arm, enthusiasm propelling her forwards. "I'm going to miss my lesson."

With heavy legs, I followed her through the door and there it was. A huge expanse of water, a huge potential for disaster.

With her free hand she pushed me sharply backwards and yanked my hair so that my face was under the water. Gasping at the cold I tried to scream, but the water hit the back of my throat.

"You sit over there, Mummy," she said, pointing to a line of white chairs. "Just wait till you see my front crawl."

My breathing ragged, I made my way to the chairs, my hand flat at the side of my face to blot out all sight of the pool.

Choking, gagging, gurgling, retching, dying. The water filled my eyes and my ears, my nose, my mouth. My heart and lungs were drowning. 'Stay still' she hissed, whacking my skull against the tiles, her bony hand squeezing tighter, tighter, around my throat.

The chair was inches away, I was almost there, but a sudden splash from the pool sent a whooshing noise through my ears. I felt the water hit the side of my leg. Without looking back, I turned and ran. Ran from the pool. Ran from the danger. Ran from my mother.

1971 - 1973

HAMILTON, LANARKSHIRE.

1

The Broken Telephone

Holding the receiver in my chubby little hand, I babbled excitedly into the mouthpiece, the words and half-words tumbling from my mouth, faster and faster, as though they were rolling off down a hill.

"You know that telephone is not even plugged in, don't you?" said my mother, Betty, without waiting for a reply as she wandered past.

But that made no difference to me. The two ornamental telephones which sat proudly on the wooden sideboard in our living room provided me with hours of entertainment. I'd chat away, quite happily, on my own, calling my grandmother, or my Uncle Jerry, or the ginger cat who lived next door but one.

Our flat, on Johnstone Street, in Hamilton, belonged to my mum's brother, Jerry, but he let us live there, rent-free. As a little girl, I thought he was incredibly and inexplicably kind. It was only when I grew older that I understood that Jerry's benevolence represented, in fact, a desperate, last-ditch attempt to drag my mother back towards a respectable way of life, and in doing so keep us together as a family. If my mother's heart was shrivelled like a prune, then Jerry, it seemed to me, had a heart big enough for the whole of Scotland. The flat itself was above a shop and had a huge stone bay window at the front. Jerry had furnished the living room for us with a black and white telly, a brown three-seater sofa, and the sideboard, with, of course, the two marvellous telephones. In the far corner, there was a partitioned area which served as a small bedroom, with a pull-down bed, a little like a large sofa bed, where we slept.

Downstairs, on the landing below, was the bathroom, decorated in that dull shade of mid-brown that was so fashionable in the early 70s. As a little girl, I loved tiptoeing down those five or six steps at night to the toilet. There was no carpet on the concrete steps, and I can still remember the feeling of the icy cold floor on the soles of my feet; at once deeply uncomfortable but oddly exhilarating. By the time I got back into bed, my feet were deliciously numb with cold, and I would hug them up into my chest, and roll myself into a little ball, until I was lulled back to sleep again.

And Jerry's generosity extended way beyond our living arrangements; he made sure that I had toys and clothes; a summer dress, a winter coat, hats, gloves, shoes and boots. Possibly I was around three years old when he turned up at the flat one winter's day carrying a red coat, fur-trimmed, with a matching muffler. My eyes widened as I opened the package, barely able to believe that this was for me.

"You look a picture, Monica," he beamed. "You're the best dressed kid on the whole street, and the prettiest too!"

My mother, I noticed, stared woodenly at the wall and

said nothing. All that week, I longed for the cold weather to come; I prayed for biting winds, numbing frosts and snow drifts, so that I could parade around the neighbourhood in my furry finery, like a pint-sized princess. And even on the warmer days, at risk of overheating, I'd button up my lovely coat and go out to play. I took to wearing it indoors too.

"You never have that coat off your back," Mum commented, in a flat sort of voice, as I hopped up onto the sofa, next to her.

I shimmied along the cushions, until my arm was touching hers, but she didn't react at all. It was though she was made of stone. Perhaps a small part of me longed for her to reach out and cuddle me, or at the very least pat my knee or ruffle my hair. But there was nothing from her. I might just as well not have been there. And yet, though I would have loved a cuddle, her behaviour didn't upset me. I was used to this lack of response; my mother had never been in any way tactile or affectionate, and so to me, it was perfectly normal. I could not, after all, miss what I had never had.

On the outside, my mother was absolutely beautiful. When I was born, in February 1968, she was 25 years old and so would be 29 by the time we were living in the flat in Hamilton with the two telephones. People in our neighbourhood used to say that she was the double of Elizabeth Taylor; long, shiny jet-black hair which she wore in a thick headband, just like Taylor. She had big, liquid blue eyes, which were heavily made-up with kohl, top and bottom. And yet they were blank and completely expressionless, as if they were made of nothing more than coloured glass. So often, I longed to see some warmth and affection in those eyes.

Mum was very fashionable, she wore high platform heels, and my own favourite was a pair of towering sandals with a strappy front, showing off her painted toes. She was celebrated, I later learned, for having the best pair of legs in Hamilton. With her heels, she'd wear flares or a short skirt with a fitted top or jumper, to show off a lovely, slim, figure. And she set it all off with large silver hooped earrings and around 20 silver bracelets which jangled on her wrist if she ever laughed. She had a showy costume ring too, with a big blue stone in the middle. And she had a deep, throaty voice, which only added to the glamour and the mystery. To me, aged four, she looked like a real film star. And in many ways, she was as distant and as inaccessible as Elizabeth Taylor herself.

* * * *

There was no particular routine to my early childhood days in the flat. Occasionally, my mother might be up very early, with me, to make my breakfast. She might even spend the morning singing and cleaning or trying on a mini skirt with a new pair of shoes; she had dozens of pairs of shoes, all piled higgledy-piggledy by the door. Once she started cleaning, she seemed to find it hard to stop, and on those days our flat gleamed and shone. The smell of polish was a reassuring one for me, because it told me that my mother was having one of her better days.

But it was far more usual for her to stay curled on the sofa deep into the afternoon, and she might not even surface for the whole day. She lay across the sofa cushions, with her knees pulled right up to her chest, covered with a faded red checked blanket. She didn't even open the curtains.

"I prefer the dark," she said, in her deep, husky voice, whenever I pulled them back.

There were days on end when the dishes piled higher and higher in the sink, the laundry basket overflowed, and the empty vodka bottles and lager cans lay scattered around the floor like tiresome guests overstaying a welcome. On those days, aged only four, I made my own breakfast, usually just milk poured clumsily into a bottle, then I got myself dressed, and amused myself making imaginary calls on the two telephones.

"Yes, yes," I gabbled to make-believe playmates. "I am playing out later. I have my new coat on. I'm just waiting for Mummy to open her eyes and let me out the front door."

Leaving the line open, I would dash to the second telephone, to shout out a quick reply: "Don't forget to bring your muffler!" before running back to the first telephone. And so on.

Those telephones provided me with hours of fun and escapism. Some days, they were the only conversations I had, and of course, they were all with myself. I was the one at both ends of the call and so I was the only human contact. At the time, it didn't bother me at all and in fact I marvelled at how lucky I was to have not one, but two, fantastic telephones at my disposal.

Those fake phones would become a metaphor for my

entire childhood; a symbol of the disparity between how things looked, and how things actually were. My mother, despite her finery and glamour, was no film star and neither was she deserving of any kind of celebrity or special status. And though, on the surface, I appeared to be a child with everything, I was lacking in the only thing that mattered; a mother who loved and cared for me.

I don't remember ever trying to wake my mother, not even when I was hungry or cold or lonely. It wasn't that I was frightened of her; she never lost her temper, and she rarely raised her voice to me. And in many ways, perhaps a show of irritation or a flash of anger would have been preferable to the terminal indifference she displayed. She wasn't maternal or affectionate or caring. And yet she wasn't mean or snappy or aggressive. She was a blank space; little more than a filmy image, floating around the flat. I had more chance of Elizabeth Taylor making my breakfast than my own mother.

What usually roused her, rather than her family's needs, was a lack of alcohol. Late at night, I found it perfectly normal to button my lovely red coat over my pyjamas and trail behind my mother on a mercy mission to buy more vodka. I thought nothing of it, in fact, I quite enjoyed the adventure in the dark. Sometimes, I'd slip my hand into hers, as she walked along the street to the off-licence, and I was struck firstly by how she did not clasp my fingers back, in the reassuring way that other adults did. But I noticed too how short her nails were; bitten right down to the quick. Although she loved to look glamorous, those ugly fingernails always let her down and gave her away. It seemed as though they were the tell-tale sign of what really lay beneath the layers of make-up and the rows of bangles.

With the vodka bottle under her arm, and without so much as a glance towards me, she'd stagger back out of the shop and then set off home, before sinking into the sofa, glassy eyed and silent and knocking back coloured pills with swigs of vodka, straight from the bottle. It was up to me to get myself into bed, and to get myself up again the next morning. I never questioned it, and I certainly never felt sorry for myself, because it was all I knew. And when my mother was on one of her benders, my maternal grandmother, Mary, usually showed up before too many days had passed, wearing her flowery apron, and bringing with her assurance and order and a wholesome smell of soap and baked biscuits. She'd buzz about the flat, tidying, cleaning, and cooking, until everything was back in order again.

"Now Monica," she'd say, patting her knees. "Jump up here and I'll tell you a nice story."

I adored my Granny. The glaring problem with her visits was that I knew they were temporary, and I was always disheartened when it was time for her to go home again.

If Mum was awake, and vaguely sober, we would visit Granny everyday ourselves. It was the only regular fixture in our otherwise chaotic yet strangely empty lives. I loved going to see my grandparents, and even though it was quite a walk for my little legs, I never complained because I knew there was a warm cuddle at the end of it. Granny always greeted us with her plump arms outstretched, her apron strings flying out behind her. I can't remember ever seeing her without her apron on and the loud flowers on the pattern seemed to shout out a welcome. That apron was like a comfort blanket for me. What you saw with Granny was what you got; she was uncomplicated, honest and loving, and the very antithesis to my mother.

On sunny days, Granny might be outside, chatting to her neighbours over the fence, her face animated, smiling, part way through a funny anecdote or a slice of gossip. If it was especially hot, she would take me to the park to find the ice-cream van, and my mother would lie out alone in her parents' back garden slathered in cooking oil with her eyes closed. She did not need a 'do not disturb' sign over her face. I knew better than that. Besides, when I had Granny looking after me, I didn't need my mother at all. Other times, Mum might disappear altogether for hours, leaving Granny and Grandpa to look after me. I loved to help Granny cook; she would lift me onto a little stool in her kitchen whilst she made mince and tatties or a chicken pie.

"You'll make a great cook yourself one day, Monica," she would say, as I stirred the pot.

My Grandpa, Eddie, was a miner by trade, a very tall thin man who, when he was not at work, was always smartly dressed. I loved standing at the window and watching for him walking down the street, after his shift had ended. Whilst Granny was making our evening meal, he'd keep me occupied playing card games or 'I Spy' and I was a captive audience.

"And so – you have the winning hand, Monica. Well done,

you beat your old Grandpa! Again!" I had no idea he was letting me win, and I'd beg to play another round. He had his own chair, next to the television, in front of the living room window. In the evenings, after we'd eaten, he would light the coal fire, and it was so snug and cosy in there; I felt absolutely at home, perversely more so than I could ever do so in the flat with my mother.

"Sit back from the fire, Monica, or you'll burn your legs," Granny would say, gently pulling my chair back a few inches.

I loved watching the flames dance and the embers as they floated off up the chimney, out into the dark night sky. Those days and nights spent with my grandparents were nourishment for my soul. I was happy there; more than that, I was safe, and I was wanted. I belonged with them.

* * * *

On Granny and Grandpa's street, there was a weekly rag and bone man, who was known to give out a lollipop or maybe a small yo-yo or a balloon, in return for a pile of old clothes. With this in mind, when I was playing outside their house one afternoon, I ran inside to search for something I could swap for a lolly. Granny was busy in the back garden, and Grandpa was at work. And so I scurried upstairs and into my aunt's bedroom and opened the wardrobe. There, hanging in front of me, was a black fur coat.

"She won't need this," I said to myself. "It's an ugly old coat. Looks like a dead cat."

It was a bit of a struggle to yank the coat down off the hook, but I managed, on tiptoes, and I made it out into the street just in time to catch the rag and bone cart, and to exchange the fur for a lollipop and a yo-yo.

"Where did you get that?" Granny asked suspiciously, with one eye on the retreating rag and bone cart, by now at the top of the street.

I shrugged, suddenly less sure of myself, the guilt flooding across my face.

"Monica?" she said sternly.

"I gave the fur coat in," I said in a small voice. "But I got a yo-yo as well!"

Granny shrieked and tore after the cart, shouting at the top of her lungs. She managed to catch up with him in the next street and when she came back, red-faced and puffed out, she was carrying the coat, by now rather bedraggled, under her arm.

"Yo-yo," she demanded, holding out her hand. "You must not take what doesn't belong to you."

It was a lesson I wouldn't forget, and my grandparents and my aunt teased me about the coat for many years.

But it seemed that my mischievous streak wasn't quite yet tamed because I was in trouble once again, some weeks later, for pinching washing off a neighbour's line and hiding it under her hedge. I then hid myself, watching her come out of the house and look around in astonishment. Of course she spotted the washing easily enough and she spotted me too. I got another telling off from Granny:

"Monica, you can't go into other people's gardens and just pull down the washing! It's not a game you know. She'll have to wash those sheets again. Good job she saw the funny side, because I wouldn't, I can tell you." But I noticed a smile playing around her lips. She could never be angry with me for long. That night, when Mum arrived to collect me, Granny pulled me in close for a goodbye embrace.

"You know that you're loved so much," she told me softly, as she planted a kiss on my head. "Don't ever forget it."

I could not have known how much I would cling to those words in the years to come; how I would turn them over in my mind with such care, like precious jewels, before placing them back, for safe keeping, inside my heart. Those words meant everything to me.

2

Charlie Mount

My father, Charlie Mount, had a stop-start presence in our lives, a little like a stomach bug or a persistent virus. We might see him every day for a week but afterwards, he would vanish for maybe a month or three months. And invariably, he left a bad feeling, like an odour, behind him.

That said, I was always over the moon to see him. He was a very smart man, and handsome too. He was 15 years older than my mother, well-spoken and polite, with fair hair and piercing blue eyes. I had inherited those same eyes, as he always loved to tell me, and equally I loved to hear it. He had shiny shoes and always wore a suit and a crisp shirt, even on weekends. Though he was not particularly tall, he was broad and imposing, and brought a presence into every room.

Just hearing his voice outside our front door sent a rush of joy through me. He'd scoop me up in his arms and twirl me around under the light, making over-exaggerated exclamations about how much I had changed.

"You've grown! At least a foot! And you're prettier than ever, so y'are!"

Dad worked as a singer, in pubs and clubs, and he usually

performed songs from eras gone by, from the fifties and the sixties. He might work away, in London or Manchester, for weeks at a time, so his homecomings were always so special to me. He sang in the flat too, he'd often pull me up onto his knee when he visited and sing: 'Ol' Blue Eyes Is Back' by Sinatra or 'Bye Bye Love' by the Everly Brothers.

"Again, again!" I clapped, bouncing on his knee in time to his toe-tapping.

It was always very late by the time he finished work and when he arrived back at the flat, he might be a little worse for wear, and it was then that it all started to go wrong. He and my mother would get into drunken arguments, mainly about other women, but often about nothing at all. Because of Dad's job, he was never short of female admirers, and whether or not he encouraged them, I don't know. The same could be said of Mum, of course. She took great care with her appearance, and she was well-known for her glamour. Perhaps they were each so self-obsessed and vain that they couldn't sustain a relationship with each other. All I knew, for certain, as a little child, was that the recipe of my mother, plus my father, plus alcohol, was a highly flammable one. Many nights, I clapped my hands over my ears to drown out the sound of them shouting and crying. The next morning, there was smashed crockery and upturned furniture in the living room, and I would catch my mother wincing and dabbing make-up over a black eye or a bruised cheekbone.

"Mummy?" I asked, my face screwed up in concern. "What's the matter?"

But she didn't reply. After that, we wouldn't see Dad for a

while. Even though he and Mum were married, they seemed to spend more time apart than together, which again, I didn't question, because it seemed like a normal arrangement to me. I missed Dad, of course, when he was away. But I didn't miss the chaos and the unease that came with him.

One warm, sticky night, in the summer of 1972, Dad came back to the flat in the early hours after a night working in the clubs, and possibly some late socialising afterwards. Mum was not asleep, and I imagine she must have been waiting for him, on the sofa, half-empty vodka bottle lazily balanced on her knee. Before long, the shouting began, the crying, the screaming, the horrible names. I clamped my hands against the sides of my head so hard that my ears hurt. But still, I could not block out the noise. I tried to sing one of my favourite songs from Dad's repertoire:

'Where are the clowns?

'Send in the clowns.'

But my voice was thin and pitiful and no match for the backdrop of rage and fury, being hammered out just a few feet away from me. Dad sounded so angry; I could visualise the spittle, flying through the air, with every insult. And then, there was an almighty crash and a scream, followed by a shattering, splintering sound. Followed by an ominous silence.

"Betty?" came Dad's voice, lower now, and suddenly wavering and unsure. "Betty?"

Scrambling to the side of the bed, I pulled on my shoes and crept, through the gloom, to the other side of the living room. I knew, immediately, what had happened, because there was a cool breeze around my legs and a big hole where the window pane had once been. My mother stood, clutching her arm, the blood already staining her sleeves, dripping down onto her skirt and splashing onto the floor. For a moment, she looked deathly pale, but then she seemed to rally a little, and she screeched:

"How could you? You put my arm through the glass! You might have killed me!"

And unbelievably, it began again. She seemed to forget about her injured arm as she pointed her finger in my father's face. Whilst they yelled at each other, I seized my chance. Pushing a chair towards the front door, I climbed up and undid the latch. And then, shoving the chair aside, I slipped out of the flat, down the stairs, and into the cold night. There was only one place, in my mind, that I could go.

"Granny," I said softly to myself. "Granny will know what to do."

It was a journey I had done many times with my mother. But never on my own. I was just four and half years old and it was a mile-and-a-half walk to Hillside Crescent, Hamilton, where my grandparents lived. Even now, looking back, I shudder when I think of that small girl, in just a flimsy nightie, walking the streets all alone at 2am. I want to reach into the tableau and scoop her into my arms and carry her the rest of the way.

But that night, all alone, I relied on the kindly glow of the streetlamps and told myself they were there to guide me and look after me. To distract myself, I tried to count them, but of course I wasn't yet at school, and when I reached number five, I was baffled. I couldn't remember what came next.

"Start again, Monica," I told myself. "Count to five again."

On and on I walked, without seeing a soul. If a car passed, or a stranger looked out of a window, I was not aware of it. Nobody stopped me or challenged me at all. My little legs grew weary and tired and yet, I told myself, this was a journey I had done so often, with my mother. Though how much longer it seemed now when I was on my own. I walked past so many houses, all in darkness, all the occupants asleep and safe in bed. I imagined all those mothers tucking their children in, reading bedtime stories, watching over them as they slept. And I felt a stab of bitterness that it could not be me. I thought of my own mother, of the black tramlines of make-up leaking down her face as she clutched her bleeding arm, and I squeezed my eyes shut tight to keep in my leaking tears.

A stray cat darted suddenly across the pavement and made me squeal in alarm. For a moment, my heart thudded against my ribs, and I considered turning back. But this – even this – was preferable to being trapped in that flat, with the noise, the violence and the fear of what might come next.

As I rounded the corner into Hillside Crescent, my pace quickened a little. I almost ran that last stretch as tears of relief and joy now streamed freely down my cheeks. I had made it. Luckily for me, in those days, people left their back doors permanently unlocked. I hadn't even considered how I was going to get into the house, or that Granny, and indeed the whole family, might be asleep in bed. When I pushed the back door, and it opened into an eerily silent house, I was perplexed.

"What now?" I wondered.

I didn't want to wake Granny and Grandpa or my aunts and uncles. Besides, I was wary of getting into trouble. I had a sudden realisation that my unscheduled visit might not go down too well with the grown-ups. What if they sent me back? Holding my breath, I tiptoed through the house and up the stairs, still without any idea of a firm plan. Hesitantly, I inched open the door to Granny and Grandpa's room, and the mellifluous sound of Grandpa's snores floated out onto the landing. Those familiar snores were like the finishing flag in a marathon. I had made it. I was here. In that second, all the adrenaline and the energy seemed to drain out of me in one big slop and I sank to the carpet, completely exhausted. Granny had a large cupboard at the end of her bed, with the door slightly ajar, and I crawled inside, using my two hands as a pillow, and fell fast asleep. It was around 5am when I was awoken, very rudely, by a torchlight in my eyes.

"She's here, she's fast asleep, poor little mite," said an unfamiliar man's voice. "Oh, she's waking up. I think she's alright."

I shrank back in terror but then spotted my Granny's face, peering over a policeman's shoulder.

"Monica!" she gasped. "What on earth are you doing in here? How did you get here? Why didn't you wake me?"

I was stiff from being curled up in the cupboard and dazed by the torch and all the attention, but Granny helped me scramble to my feet and she pulled me into a hug on the edge of the bed.

"Let me look at you," she kept saying, patting my arms and legs. "Let me check you're all in one piece."

Later, over a hot cup of tea, as I told the police the story of how I had walked the mile-and-a-half, on my own, during the night, an uncomfortable silence fell in the kitchen. Granny and Grandpa exchanged looks that spoke volumes and were beyond my four and a half years.

"We'll make sure this doesn't happen again, officer," said Granny. "We'll keep her safe, I promise."

For my part, I was hugely impressed with myself for making the journey and finding my way and counting all those streetlamps. It is only now, looking back, that my heart breaks for my childhood self, and at the fear and desperation I must have felt, to drive me to such drastic action.

3

Hillside Crescent

It was only a few days later when my mother announced that we were leaving the flat, for a new home.

"Where?" I asked excitedly. "Where are we going?"

"We're moving into your Granny's road," Mum replied dully. "Hillside Crescent."

I couldn't believe my luck. I ran around the flat collecting my clothes and toys and throwing them into bags. By now, Dad had done another disappearing act, off to London, I was told, to sing in the clubs. But I took one look at my mother's bandaged arm, with splotches of red staining the dressing, and I shuddered. Still, nothing could keep the smile off my face for long; the idea of living so close to Granny and Grandpa was a dream come true. I wondered whether I might even hatch a plan to live with them permanently; my mother was, after all, so often asleep or drunk and there was a distinct possibility I could move in with them without her objecting. Or even noticing.

Our new place, opposite Granny's, was two storeys. We had our own bathroom and there was a kitchen, an upstairs living room and two bedrooms. On the stairs, there was a runner carpet, just like at Granny's. Clapping my hands together, I ran from room to room, thrilled with my new home. Again, Uncle Jerry stepped in, taking over the painting and decorating. The rooms were mainly painted a neutral beige but one of the bedrooms had large pink polka dots on the walls, which looked like measles to me, and I asked if I could have a different bedroom.

"Course you can," Jerry chuckled.

Mum always slept downstairs on a sofa, so curiously did not ever use a bed. She rarely went into a bedroom at all. The second bedroom therefore was a spare room and was smaller; just enough space for a double bed with a white bedspread, embroidered with flowers, on the top. The curtains were always closed.

"You're not to go in that room," Mum told me firmly. "Not ever!"

It wasn't like her to lay down any rules or make any demands of me and so the words struck a chord and stayed with me. I often wondered what was so special about a plain bedroom, with measles on the walls, and space enough only for a bed and a small set of drawers. But I never found out.

Jerry was kept busy, bringing us a sofa and a dining table and chairs. The ornamental telephones, sadly, had remained in the old flat, and I knew I would miss the hours of silly games I'd played. But the regret was outweighed by my delight at the new house. And Uncle Jerry brought new toys and gifts, including a bracelet with my name on it. I gazed at it and announced it was the loveliest thing I had ever set eyes on.

"Thanks, Uncle Jerry," I beamed. "Thank you so much!"

"You're welcome, Monica," he replied, with a big smile of his own. "We'll see you every day now."

And he was right. Granny was round every morning, making sure that I was up and dressed and had eaten breakfast. Even now, aged four and a half, I carried my bottle around with milk inside. Nobody had ever taken it from me or suggested that I was too old for a bottle, and I certainly wasn't about to give it up myself. In the afternoons, I'd often go to Granny's to wait for my aunts and uncles and Grandpa as they arrived home from work. My mum was one of seven children, and Granny still had a full house, with some of her younger children not yet flown the nest. I loved the hustle and bustle there, the noise and the laughter. It was in stark contrast to the loneliness of my own home.

What I loved most at Granny's was sitting on the window ledge, in the kitchen, and watching Uncle Jerry working on his orange Capri car on the path outside. He loved that car and was forever tinkering with the engine or polishing the bonnet. The smell of petrol and oil floated up, through the open kitchen window, and I pulled it down, into my lungs, like an elixir. I hankered after that smell because it made me think of Jerry, and kindness, and safety. Even now, when I get the occasional whiff of petrol, I am transported back to that window ledge, and to Jerry, and to happy times. In the background, I could hear the click-click of the electric meter on the kitchen wall, and, as a special treat, I was allowed to feed coins in the slot myself and listen to them drop with a satisfying clunk into its bowels.

"Ten pence, twenty, thirty," Granny taught me, pointing at the coins in my hand.

When Mum was not lying under her red blanket, in a stupor, she loved to socialise. After several days, virtually comatose, she would suddenly be filled, quite inexplicably, with a new and mercurial energy.

"Come on Monica!" she'd shout. "Help me dig out my pink platforms, I'm in the mood to party!"

She liked to dress up, in make-up and fashionable clothes, and of course there was always a bottle of vodka involved in the planning. She was like a wind-up toy, who suddenly came alive when alcohol was added to the mix. When she was getting ready to go out, she would let me blow dry her hair, and, as I brushed it, she would pick up her compact mirror and pull a funny face to make me laugh. For a treat, I was allowed to apply the hairspray too, and I'd say:

"Tell me when to stop!"

I sprayed and sprayed until my little finger was aching on the nozzle, but Mum never said a word. By the time she finally shouted "Stop!" her hair was as solid as a brick and we were both giggling hysterically.

Those were rare moments, and I treasured those snippets of joy. Yet even they were bittersweet too; glimpses of how life might have been, of how it could have been. Of how she should have been, as my mother.

She had a quirky little move, a characteristic, which always surfaced after the first few drinks. She would throw her head back and flick her eyes skyward, whilst kicking up one leg too. It was whimsical and eccentric and always made me laugh.

Again, a chance to see what life might have been like – if only she had been able to stop at a few drinks.

On those outings, we might visit the neighbours, or friends further across the town. I loved those times because there were invariably children I could play with. One of my neighbours, Liz, was my age, and we became firm pals over the years. We had so much fun on those nights. But Mum would also take me with her to visit various, vague associates, and she was never very forthcoming with their details.

"Where are we going?" I'd ask, as I put on a pair of sandals that Granny had bought for me.

"Off to see posh paws," was her standard reply.

It was one of her favourite expressions which made me giggle when I was small, but now I see that she was dodging the question. We'd go to a house I didn't recognise, and Mum would sit and drink with a few people whilst I occupied myself quietly, with the bribe of sweets or a colouring book and new felt pens. I'd let myself out too, into the street, and find other kids to play with. I was used to making my own entertainment, thanks to the two telephones in our old flat. And clearly, I was used to looking after myself.

Other times, we'd visit men I didn't know, and she would leave me downstairs, whilst they went off, carrying the vodka, to another room. Again, because this was normal, I never questioned or complained about these trips. I certainly didn't see the implications of what she was doing. When we visited the strange men, it got very late sometimes, and I longed to be home in bed and fast asleep like other children. But I knew better than to try and hurry her up. When it was a choice between me or the vodka, the vodka always won. Perhaps I did wonder why she didn't leave me with Granny and Grandpa, instead of dragging me out on her mystery jaunts. Now of course I realise that she didn't want them to know what she was up to. After these visits, she always had money for a bag of chips, pop, and a couple of bottles of vodka. We had a brief window, of maybe half an hour, when she was chatty and smiley and funny.

"I'll be on the bones of my arse after I've bought you these chips," she'd say, and I'd snigger delightedly at the swear word.

And then, she would swig off the dregs of the vodka, and slump into yet another daze, lasting for the rest of the week. Her good mood evaporated faster than her hairspray. I learned to enjoy my chips and my fizzy pop and not to ask too many questions.

Later that year, in September 1972, I started school at St John's Primary, just a short walk from my home. Granny would usually walk me to school, or occasionally Mum would do it instead.

When I came home, more often than not, I sat on my own, watching the TV which was on all day, regardless of whether anyone was watching it. Mum might be asleep on the sofa, or she might be scrunched up, under her blanket, staring right through the screen. The background buzz droning endlessly on, was the soundtrack to my childhood. In those first few weeks at school, if I had done an especially impressive painting, or I had fallen and grazed my knee in the playground, I fell into the trap of trying to share my news with my mother.

"Look Mummy!" I would say. "See this? I painted Granny

and Grandpa. I did it all on my own." But she barely turned her head. In the half-light, with the curtains drawn, and with smears of yesterday's make-up around her eyes, she looked almost ghoulish.

"Mmm," she said in a neutral, absent voice. "Mmm."

I felt as though I could press a button for a standard response. I never got anything more from her – or anything less. She was robotic in the way she parented me. There was no attachment, no bond there at all, and as a result, there was nothing from my side either. I was not an affectionate or an expressive child and most of my conversations took place inside my own head. As my first year at school progressed, I became a self-reliant little girl, savvy and streetwise. I was used to my own company and when I got lonely, I needed only to knock on Granny's door. In the evenings, after the washing up was done, and the daylight was fading, Granny would say to me:

"Home time now, sweetheart, you have school in the morning."

My face always fell at those words. It was only a short walk back home and, as I stared at the blank windows in the street, the closed doors and the locked gates, I was reminded of my mother and her shuttered face. Always, I found her on the sofa, in the exact same spot, fixated on the telly as though she was under a technological spell. And even very late at night, way after the test card was shown, our TV remained on. Much like my mother, it was switched on. It was there. But there was little else besides.

4

The Incident

In July 1973, Dad had a few nights off work, and he came home to be with us. I always loved to have him around, despite the inevitable arguments between him and my mother. Besides, with Granny just over the road now, I knew I had a refuge if he became violent again. Her house was a sanctuary to me, on so many levels. One warm evening, that same week, Mum announced that we were off out to see some friends.

"I've got you a bag of Woolworths pick and mix," she told me. "And here, there's a new colouring book in this bag. That will keep you quiet."

I swung my legs on the edge of her bed as she slicked on layers of dark eye make-up and lipstick. I was allowed to blast her with hair spray for my usual treat.

"Tell me when to stop," I said.

But though I was laughing and half choking on the fumes, she screwed up her eyes and said nothing, until her hair was set solid like concrete.

"You look beautiful Mummy," I told her.

And I meant it. Perhaps it was because she was smiling,

maybe it was because Dad was home, or it could have been the balmy summer weather. Possibly it was a combination of all three. But I had a good feeling as I skipped along the pavement that night. I heard the vodka bottles clinking inside the carrier bag slung over Mum's arm. I saw the tell-tale bitten fingernails. I noticed her throwing back her head and kicking her leg. But I ignored all of those warning signs and focussed on the joy of the evening ahead.

"Bet I can skip faster than you," said Dad, playfully pushing me out of the way, and I laughed and pushed him back.

This was how it was supposed to be; a little girl with a mummy and a daddy either side of her. No arguments. No tension. No tears. I felt so happy. I didn't know the people we were visiting, and they had no children, but I had my bag of goodies, so I was quite content. It was a small house, not far from ours, and I remember there were at least two other guests there. I kept myself busy drawing and lining my sweets up on the table for a while. As the night wore on, I grew really tired. I was still only five years old, and I was struggling to stay awake so late.

"Come here," said Dad, seeing me rubbing my eyes.

He held his arms out and pulled me onto his knee.

"Give us a song Charlie," said one of the female guests, and Dad smiled. He launched into a Sinatra set as I sat on his knee, looking around me at the half-filled glasses on the table, the sticky patches of spillages, and the large slate ashtray, overflowing with cigarette ends. As Dad crooned, I heard my mother coming down the stairs, on her way back from the bathroom.

"Come on, Monica," she said, standing in the doorway. "Come up to the bathroom with me."

I was comfortable on Dad's knee, almost dozing, and I didn't want to move. I shook my head sleepily.

"Come on," she said again, this time with an edge to her tone.

I didn't reply, but Dad stopped singing and said: "Go with your Mum, Monica, there's a good girl. Go on up to the toilet."

The music came back on, louder than before, and I slid off Dad's knee and walked over to slip my hand into Mum's. Step by step we went, up to the landing, my small hand in hers. I looked at her bitten nails, her hair, slightly askew now despite the spray, her make-up a little smudged. She didn't speak at all. But my hand was in hers and so I was safe, wasn't I? There was a glass panel in the bathroom door, frosted so that nobody could peer through.

We went inside and Mum closed the door.

All safe.

The toilet was facing me, with the sink next to it, and above that a small window, again in misted glass. The bath was next to the sink. On the window ledge was a line of perfume bottles, in coloured glass, and my first instinct was to reach out to play with them and rearrange them in order of colours. I was wondering idly whether I might be allowed a quick spray of a pretty pink bottle, when Mum suddenly flicked on the bath taps, and, with the water gushing out on full, she pushed me, roughly, towards the side of the bath.

Confused, and slightly alarmed, I said nothing.

I glanced back at the door panel and my image was fractured and distorted into something sinister in the misted glass.

Wasn't I supposed to be in here to go to the toilet? Surely, I wasn't expected to have a bath in a stranger's house and in the middle of the night too? Was everything quite as it seemed? As the questions whirled around my head, Mum clasped both of her hands around my neck and squeezed very tightly. I let out a small squeal of protest, more of a frightened whimper, at what might lay ahead. Lifting one hand she shoved me again sharply, backwards over the bath, and yanked my hair so that my face was under the stream of water. Gasping at the cold I tried to shout, but the water hit the back of my throat.

"Mummy!" I screamed, but I wasn't sure whether the voice was in my head or out loud.

The water filled my eyes and my ears, my nose and my mouth. My heart and lungs were ballooning, pumped up like beach balls, ready to explode. I felt as though I was drowning, standing up. With all my strength, I wriggled and struggled, and I managed to move a little, so that my face was half turned towards the bottom of the bath. Now, the water ran icy cold down my hair, my neck, and under my clothes.

"Stay still," she hissed, whacking my skull against the tiles, her bony hand squeezing tighter, tighter, around my throat.

Choking, gagging, gurgling, retching, dying…my lungs swelled and swelled until they were bursting out of my chest. I was not sure whether I was still alive. Yet I could feel the cold water, I heard my heart clattering against my ribs, and I could just make out the distant, all too distant, sound of the music and the laughter downstairs. Was this the end for me, Monica Mount, aged five years and five months?

****

In the years which followed, the trauma of my mother trying to drown me in a stranger's bathroom would come back to haunt me like a persistent ghost, gnawing at the lining of my brain like a rodent. I would ask myself if it was planned, and if so, what was her end aim? And why on earth, unless she was actively hoping to be caught out, would she attack me with a room full of people downstairs? Was it an act of revenge against my father, who had earlier been entertaining another woman with his singing? Was it an act of hatred against me because she resented being a mother?

I wondered whether she put the taps on to drown out the noise of my screaming, or if this was a depraved form of waterboarding, and she had specifically chosen this cruel combination of drowning and strangling for her young daughter. I was unsure whether it was planned, or spontaneous, whether it was even a conscious act. Possibly she was drunk, probably she was out of her mind? More than anything, I could not accept that a mother, my mother, the one person who was supposed to look after me and keep me from harm, would try to kill me.

"Why? Why? Why?" I asked myself.

In equal measure, I blamed her, I hated her, I pitied her. I wanted her punished, but more than that, I wanted her love. Oh, how I wanted her love. I needed answers to all these questions. But there were none.

Perhaps fortunately, as a small child, my subconscious blocked out the horror of the aftermath. My memory went into some kind of temporary hibernation, like a frightened animal, unable to face the harsh reality of the cold winter. And so, I remember nothing after the attack. I have no idea how or when I was rescued from the bathroom or what happened to me in the days which followed. Without doubt, I was not allowed to return home with my mother. I presume that my father, or one of the house guests, heard my screams and came to save me. The police, and social services, must have been called soon after.

1973 - 1985

EAST KILBRIDE

5

The Stewart Family

When my memory reawakens, some days later, I am standing on the doorstep of an average three-bedroom terraced house, with brown wooden panelling on the front and a brown fence around a small front garden. The houses were grouped in fours along the street and looked much the same as each other. In my hand was my baby's bottle, half-filled with milk. And standing at my side was a female social worker. I had no suitcase, no bag, no clothes or toys or even a teddy bear. My only possession was my trusty bottle, which, aged five and a half, I still carried around like a comfort blanket.

"Ready, Monica?" asked the social worker brightly, and I nodded in reply, though in truth I had no idea what I was supposed to be ready for.

She tapped on the door, and it opened so quickly that I presumed the lady had been standing behind it, waiting for our arrival.

"This," said the social worker, ushering me inside with a small flourish, "is Mrs Teresa Stewart."

I had no clue who Mrs Stewart was or why I had come to

see her. I had no clue, for that matter, who the social worker was either. Mrs Stewart had shoulder length dark hair with a slight curl, which was pulled back into a tidy bun. She wore a skirt with a modest split in the side and a plain jumper. She was, in every way, a smart, neat, no-nonsense person. But she had a warm face, with kindness in her eyes, and so when she extended her hand to me, I offered her mine in return.

"Let me show you where you're going to sleep, Monica," she said. "And then we'll sort out some clothes for you."

I followed her upstairs, my little knees knocking together and my heart thrashing against my chest. What was this place? Who on earth was Mrs Stewart? Where were my Granny and Grandpa and my wonderful Uncle Jerry? Where were my father and mother? Imperfect, yes. Flawed, definitely. Wicked, most likely. But they were my family. They were all I had. As we reached the top of the stairs, Mrs Stewart turned to me and nodded at the bottle in my hand.

"I don't think a big girl like you needs a baby's bottle," she said. "Do you?"

"Yes, I do," I replied boldly, determined to stand up for my beloved bottle.

I was used to speaking my mind and I was not used to adults challenging me like this. But before I had a chance to argue my case, she had snatched the bottle out of my hand and into hers.

"And we'll have no backchat. We don't like backchat, do we?" she added rhetorically.

I muttered something under my breath, biting back the

tears. Without my bottle, I had nothing from home. Nothing familiar. Later, I would find it in the bin outside, the casing cracked and the milk yellow and curdled. The bottle was my last connection with my family. And now, it was gone.

* * * *

It was late afternoon when there was a commotion in the hallway and Mrs Stewart smiled brightly and said:

"That will be the other children back from school."

I shrank back into the corner as Mrs Stewart introduced me to one older teenage boy and one much older girl. There was a little boy too, about my age, who hid behind his bigger siblings when he spotted me.

"Sharon, Steven, Gordon – this is Monica," she said. "Monica Mount."

They looked almost as confused as I was. It seemed that my arrival was a surprise for them as it was for me. When Mrs Stewart went off into the kitchen, Sharon turned to me and curled her lip.

"Who are you?" she asked in disgust. "Where did you come from?"

My heart sank into my shoes, and I trembled with fear. I didn't know if a reply was expected, and I didn't dare to attempt one. Like a frightened animal, I longed to crawl under a rock and hide away.

"I'm glad you girls are getting along, because you'll be sharing a bed at first," said Mrs Stewart, reappearing behind me. "And I'm sure Sharon will fill you in on everything you need to know here."

My jaw gaped. How could I possibly share a bed with her? Sharon was around sixteen years old, she wore glasses and had brown hair in a Purdy style, flicked out at the sides. She was only about five feet tall but broad and absolutely solid, and to me, the tiniest and most fragile of five-year-olds, she was like a fire-breathing ogre. I could not have been more frightened of the Loch Ness monster himself.

"Great," Sharon snapped sarcastically, throwing her school bag onto the carpet.

Our evening meal was a plate piled high with wholesome food, and I stared at the sheer amount in wonder. I had never had such a big serving in my entire life.

"What's the matter with you?" asked Sharon. "Never seen potatoes before? Or what?"

At home, I would maybe have milk in my bottle for breakfast and snack on sweets throughout the day. I might eat with Granny in the evenings, but always just a small portion, and she would mash it into a bowl for me so that I didn't need to chew. Or if I was with Mum, we would either skip mealtimes completely, or call in at the chippy. Certainly, I was not used to huge and intimidating dinners such as this. I was worrying about how I was going to manage, when there seemed to be a temporary reprieve, and everyone bowed their heads and joined their hands together. I gazed, wide-eyed, around the table.

"For what we are about to receive, may the Lord make us truly thankful," said Mrs Stewart.

The entire family mumbled a reply and then tucked in around me, chewing loudly, reaching across for more potatoes, more gravy, more carrots. To me, it seemed like gluttonous excess. Even the smell made me nauseous.

"Eat up, Monica," said Mrs Stewart briskly. "We don't waste food. It's a sin to waste food."

I pushed my dinner around my plate, nibbling on as much as I could. But I could feel my stomach swelling and grumbling. I just wasn't used to this, and neither was my digestive system.

Later, I would look back on social services reports from that time and learn that I had severe malnutrition and I was painfully undernourished and underweight when I was taken into foster care. I struggled to eat and digest solid food and for much of my early years my meals had been liquid or mashed up. At five years of age, I was not used to food. It was that simple. And so introducing it now, and so brutally too, was a shock to my system.

"I don't feel very well," I said quietly. "I can't eat."

Mrs Stewart made a begrudging remark about today being an exception, because I was a new arrival, and thankfully I was allowed to leave the table.

Upstairs there were three bedrooms, one for Mrs Stewart and her husband, one for the boys and one for the girls. In my new bedroom there was a single bed and a set of bunk beds in the corner. The plan was for me to share the bed with Sharon, temporarily.

"We have two other foster children who will be leaving us this week and then you can have a bunk bed," Mrs Stewart explained.

I didn't know what 'foster children' were and I didn't ask.

I looked around the room and I swallowed back the tears. I just wanted to be back at home. At the window, there were thick brown curtains which stole away all of the light, casting a gloom over the entire room and over me too. There was a brown speckled carpet and white candlewick eiderdowns on the beds. It was dated, as though I had stepped back in time, far away from Hillside Crescent, and I hated all of it.

"You'd best be no trouble at night," Sharon said, as I pulled a borrowed nightie over my head.

Little did she know that I had wet the bed pretty much every night since I had stopped wearing nappies. I was so frightened of how she might react, that I slid under the covers and forced my eyes open wide, determined not to sleep a wink.

"Never forget you are loved," I repeated to myself silently. "Never forget."

They were Granny's words, but they sounded so hollow and long ago now. Just after 9.30pm, I heard the back door slam downstairs and then footsteps on the stairs and on the narrow landing outside. When the bedroom door swung open, I was astonished to see, in the half light, a man who looked just like Santa Claus.

"This is Mr Stewart, your foster father," said Mrs Stewart, appearing at his shoulder.

I couldn't help but smile. I half expected him to dump a sack full of presents onto the carpet. He had fuzzy white hair and a long white beard. He was stocky, with small, beady eyes that twinkled through the darkness.

"Well, Monica," he said, in a stiff, warning voice. "I hope we'll have no trouble from you."

The door closed and the fantasy was shattered. The moment he spoke, I realised Mr Stewart was no Father Christmas. He was not here to spread joy or goodwill. I remembered the ornamental telephones, and all my hours of chatting to people who simply were not there. I remembered my mother laughing as I applied her hairspray. And then I saw her sullen and blank, lying on the sofa, swigging from a vodka bottle. I knew already that things were not always as they seemed. Appearances could be deceptive, then and now. It seemed, sadly, I could not even rely on Santa.

6

New Shoes

The next morning, after the older ones had left for school, Mrs Stewart opened a large cupboard in the hallway and pulled out assorted piles of jumpers, skirts, and blouses, in every size and colour imaginable. They were mostly, though, black, navy or grey, and all rather worn and tatty. From a drawer, she plucked out a handful of socks and grey-white knickers.

"Pick out your size," she said, as though she was offering me a gift. "First of all, you need a uniform for school and five changes of underwear."

Gingerly, I held up the clothes, some with visible mending, others with small holes, until we found a blouse and skirt to fit me.

"We still need a couple of jumpers and a coat," she frowned. "You're so small, that's the problem. Come on. We're going out."

We arrived soon after at a church hall where there seemed to be a permanent jumble sale along the back wall. I wilted inside as she picked out the ugliest specimens; scratchy woollen jumpers and a horrible, frumpy coat, all of which, to me, seemed far too big and shapeless on my slight frame. I had a knot of dread in my stomach that grew tighter and tighter with every minute.

"Right, shoe shop next," she said. "We always insist on new shoes, Mr Stewart and I. Always."

My heart lifted a little. I'd left my favourite pair of shoes behind at home, patent leather with a small swirl on the front, a gift from Granny, and I wondered if Mrs Stewart would let me pick out a pair exactly like those. But inside the shop, she picked up a cheap and clumpy pair of black shoes with a thick foam wedge underneath. They looked more like plastic bricks than footwear to me. My heart sank back down.

"We'll take these," she told the shop assistant.

"Oh, good choice, they won't wear out," replied the assistant knowledgeably. "They'll last forever."

She turned to me and winked:

"You'll still be wearing these when you leave school!"

My heart sank even further. The shoes were so heavy and cumbersome that I could barely lift my feet. They looked like black weights dangling on the end of my skinny legs. Even worse, they were so hideously ugly that the idea of wearing them out in public was mortifying.

"Don't like them," I grumbled. "They're bloody awful."

Mrs Stewart drew in a sharp breath and apologised profusely to the shop assistant.

"A foster child," she said primly, by way of explanation. "A new arrival. Yet to learn some manners, I'm afraid. I do apologise."

I snorted. I was used to saying just what I thought. My

mother had never worried too much about manners, her own or mine, and I had picked up lots of colourful language thanks to those night-time trips all over the city. I wasn't actually sure which words were out of bounds.

"Really Monica, you will have to learn to speak nicely, or we will have to wash your mouth out with carbolic soap," said Mrs Stewart as we walked back home.

I screwed up my nose at the thought of it. Did these people actually eat soap? But far more disturbing than the threat of a soapy meal, was the bag with the nasty shoes inside.

"You start your new school tomorrow," Mrs Stewart continued. "I'll help you lay out your uniform this once. After that, I'll expect you to do it yourself."

That evening, Mr Stewart was on a night shift, so he was at home for the meal, and we all gathered around the dining table to eat together at 5pm prompt. He joined his hands to signal the start of grace, and this time, I had picked up enough to be able to copy the others. There were seven children in total; a mix of foster children and the Stewarts' own three children.

"Monica, I want every scrap of food eaten," said Mr Stewart, fixing me with a concentrated stare. "Each morsel is a gift from God. Don't waste a single mouthful."

I did my best with the vegetables and the potatoes, but the meat was simply too tough for my teeth. I wasn't accustomed to chewing my food like this.

"Monica!" he snapped, and I jumped in alarm as though he had stung me with a cattle prod. "Eat your meat!"

I was unsure whether the meal was too bulky or too rich,

but as I made heavy work of a chunk of lamb chop, I felt my stomach roiling. Then, I felt a tell-tale tightening of my throat, and I knew that I was going to be sick. Dashing from the table, I ran to the bathroom and vomited back my entire meal. Gasping, I turned on the tap and took a gulp of cold water. Then, I heard Mr Stewart thundering up the stairs after me.

"Bedroom!" he said, his eyes glinting with either anger or anticipation, or perhaps a twisted mixture of both.

I scurried into the bedroom like a field mouse and cowered on my side of the single bed.

"Pants down, skirt off," he ordered.

Swallowing down my alarm, I pulled off my clothes and he swung me smartly over his knee so that I was facing the floor. When his hand made contact with my bare flesh I yelped in agony. His hands felt so big, and so painful, I imagined they were huge paddles made of leather.

"Ow!" I screamed. "Ow! Please! Ow!"

His hand whacked down on my backside, again and again, until the pain seemed to consume me entirely. My whole body was stinging and crying out in protest. I was aware, through my tears, of Mrs Stewart standing at the doorway, wringing her hands.

"Enough, Bob! Enough!" she shouted.

And thankfully, mercifully, the blows stopped. My backside was so raw and sore that I could not even sit down afterwards. Even in bed, that night, I could not lay down comfortably.

"Move over!" Sharon hissed, with a sharp elbow into my ribs.

But as it grew dark outside, I didn't worry about Sharon or Mr Stewart or the new school or the loss of my home or my family. I didn't even worry about the bruises or the beating. All I could think of were those disgusting black shoes. They loomed large in my dreams, two monstrous bricks, each heavy enough to drag me down and drag me under.

* * * *

At 8.30am the next morning, I walked, with the other children, to the end of the street, up a set of steps, and along the road to my new school. My new shoes were like concrete blocks welded onto my ankles. As I took my first tentative steps into the schoolyard, I felt like everyone was looking at me. It seemed to me as though every conversation stopped, every skipping rope paused mid-air, every football froze, mid-kick.

"It's the shoes, the bloody shoes," I muttered to myself, kicking at the ground.

I stood out like a sore thumb, and I knew it. I felt so uncomfortable in the second-hand uniform and the musty old duffle coat that Mrs Stewart had chosen for me. The coat was several sizes too big, and it hung from me and flapped like a tent. As we made our way into the classroom, I kept my eyes fixed on the floor and my arms tightly clasped across my chest. I was hunched over so much that I was almost folding in on myself. I felt like a wilting flower, my stem bending and breaking, as I cried out silently for nourishment. I just wanted to hide away; to disappear. Sneaking glances at all the other children, I felt a swell of longing. I wanted their shoes and their coats. I wanted their mothers and their fathers. I wanted their lives, and not mine.

"Monica," smiled my teacher brightly. "Welcome to the class."

With that, all eyes were on me. I felt so exposed. I mumbled a reply and took a chair. To the outsider, the differences were probably very subtle. I had long, fair-brown hair, worn in a bow. I had the regulation white school socks, always falling down round my ankles. A little scruffy, a little pale, a little thin, but no doubt I looked much like any other kid. Yet to me, and, I was sure, to the other children, I was clearly marked out as an outsider. The gulf between me and them was enormous, and though I desperately wanted to bridge it, I had no idea where to start. My only solution was to hunch further over my desk, bringing my shoulders up and my face down, until I was the shape of a sad letter C. If I could have pulled a curtain around my desk and chair, and cowered behind it, then I would have done so gladly. I felt somehow diminished, as if I was lesser than everyone else, as if my physical size was a direct reflection of my worth.

"I'm sure you'll settle in soon," said my teacher, handing me a name tag for my coat hook.

I nodded glumly. She could not have begun to understand the level of despair, rising within me, like a dangerous tide. At playtime, I stood and watched the other girls playing hopscotch and skipping. Part of me wanted to join in. But I was also very used to being on my own. After all, I had lost everyone who was dear to me, my parents, my grandparents, my aunts and uncles. And so finding a friend to play hopscotch with was somewhat unimportant and way down the list. And yet, as I gazed at the children laughing and playing, my heart ached. Finding a friend was, in fact, very important indeed. Hopscotch suddenly seemed vital. There were two opposing sides to my character, often wrestling with each other, and I struggled to make sense of them. I was a loner, and yet I craved company. I hunched over, I hid myself away, but I longed for affection and attention. The conflict didn't stop there. I swore and I answered back, yet I was crippled with a lack of self-confidence. At school, in class, I was withdrawn and quiet and yet there was also a fierce spark in me. I wanted to show that I could not be cowed, at least, not completely. So when one of my classmates eyed my shoes with distaste and whispered something to her pal, I prodded her on the shoulder and said:

"What's the matter?"

"Your shoes," she said, with a giggle. "They're horrible."

The humiliation stung, but I prodded her again and said:

"Your face. It's horrible!"

It was a survival instinct; a basic urge to fight back, to stand up for myself, and to keep my spirit alive. No matter if the whole world was against me, I would not be snuffed out without a battle. In the months and years to come, I would rely on that spark, more and more. As the world around me fell apart and turned on me, and I could trust nobody, I would cling to that inner flicker and I would somehow learn to cope.

Never forget you are loved, Monica.

That evening, as she was making supper for the older ones,

Mrs Stewart called me into the kitchen to help. "You can butter the toast," she told me, handing me a knife. "And there's a pot of jam in the bottom cupboard, just there."

I was very pleased to help out. I loved being in the kitchen, it reminded me of Granny and her flowery apron. I wondered if we would bake biscuits and if I might be allowed to cut out the shapes with animal-shaped cutters, like I did with Granny. I was lost in my memories as I picked up the jar of jam and to my horror it slipped right through my hands and smashed onto the tiled floor.

"Oh shit! I'm sorry!" I gasped. "I really am!"

Mrs Stewart glared at me as she swept the splinters into a dustpan.

"You swore and you dropped the jam," she said in a voice heavy with regret and judgement. "Two sins. Just wait until Mr Stewart gets home."

My backside was still sore from the previous evening, and I knew exactly what was coming. The evening wore on and, in many ways, the wait was the worst part of it all. The anticipation was unbearable.

Mr Stewart was a security worker at a big factory nearby, and his shift usually ended at 9.30pm. Other times, he worked nights. But I couldn't tell the time, so that was little help to me. I was packed off to bed, now in the top bunk of the bunkbeds in the girls' room. There was a vacancy because another girl had moved on. In my child's mind I hoped, fervently, that it might be my turn to move on before 9.30pm. It was my only chance of escape.

I waited and waited, and then, it happened. I lay frozen

with fear as the back door opened downstairs. I heard the heavy footsteps, thirteen stairs in all, nearer and nearer. With each step, my heart thumped a little faster.

"Out of bed," said Mr Stewart calmly.

He didn't raise his voice. He didn't need to. I was made to lift up my nightdress – I was expressly forbidden from wearing underwear in bed – and then the beating began. The giant hands, the heavy breath above me, the searing pain, the screaming sobs.

"Right Bob, enough. Enough!"

Mrs Stewart stood in the doorway, twisting her hands, and it signalled the end of my torture. For now. The minutes dragged by and I could tell that the little girl, in the bottom bunk below me, was already fast asleep, but I felt wide-awake and unsettled. To occupy myself, I began composing a little song.

In a big house in a green field
Far far away!
In a garden with my family
Far far away!

I sang softly, almost under my breath, so that nobody would hear. But then, I heard a voice at the doorway.

"Go to sleep!" hissed Mr Stewart. "Nobody wants to hear your voice!"

7

My First Weekend

When the weekend came, I was allowed to play outside with the other children. That Saturday morning, we went into the woods, at the end of the street, and we played hide and seek for hours. For a while, I forgot about Mr Stewart and his huge, cruel hands. I pushed all thoughts of my mother and my Granny to the back of my mind. And I had such fun ducking down behind grasses or shinning up trees. I was a quick runner, even though I was small, and so I was easily able to dart away from the older children.

"Coming ready or not!"

In the woods, I had a glimpse of how it might be to belong; to be a part of a real family, of a wider community, and I loved it. As we made our way back to the house, I noticed a motor home parked at the end of the Stewarts' driveway.

"That's for holidays," one of the older kids told me. "We go away every summer in the van."

I had never been on a holiday, ever. It sounded so exotic. And though I was desperate to leave this miserable house, and this strange family, I was also curious to go away on holiday in this funny caravan with wheels. I wondered what it might be like to sleep inside the motor home, to wake up by the seaside or in a forest. My next thought was of my Granny, and I felt horribly disloyal and confused.

Because it was Saturday, Mr Stewart was home again in the evening, and we gathered around the table at 5pm to say grace before a ham pie was served. It smelled delicious, but I knew there was no way I could digest the thick chunks of ham. Without looking up, I sensed Mr Stewart's eyes drilling through me. I shifted uneasily on my seat and swallowed as much as I could manage. But each mouthful seemed to last forever, and my jaw ached and creaked with the effort.

Somehow, I managed to keep the pie down until we were excused from the table. The minute Mr Stewart gave the word, I dashed upstairs and vomited the contents of my stomach into the toilet. Flushing again and again, I realised with a growing anxiety that the toilet was blocked with pieces of undigested ham, which looked to me like chopped up body parts. I flushed again but they floated back up and stared stubbornly at me from the bowl, like pieces of human flesh. Still dizzy with nausea, and seized with a clammy panic, I looked around in desperation. I didn't know what to do. I closed the toilet lid and opened it again, wishing for a miracle. But they were still there. My stomach still churned as I crept from the bathroom and into my bedroom and climbed up to my bunk. Just a few minutes later came the inevitable order to assemble on the landing.

"Line up!" Mr Stewart demanded.

We did as he instructed, oldest to youngest, in height order, so that I was on the very end.

"Who was sick in the toilet?" he asked, smacking together his lips. I could imagine him salivating at the prospect of doling out more punishment.

"It'll be her," Sharon hissed. "She's always throwing her guts up."

Mr Stewart ignored the tip and instead asked each one, in turn, starting with the oldest and tallest.

"Were you sick in the toilet?"

"Were you sick in the toilet?"

"Were you sick in the toilet?"

It was prolonging the agony, and I knew it was best simply to own up. But I couldn't. I was so scared; I didn't even think I could speak. Before he reached me, he stood back, rather theatrically, and said:

"You do know I have a lie detector test? The culprit will be easily identified and harshly punished when the test results come in."

My now empty stomach did a somersault of fear. I felt my palms sweating and my eyes brimming with tears. Mr Stewart leaned down and put his face close to mine. I could see the pock marks on his nose, the tiny, beady eyes, the white bristles of his beard.

"So, Monica," he said, dragging out each syllable as though my name was made of stretchy gum.

I did not realise it at the time, but of course the entire thing was a farce. He knew it was me. I knew it was me. Everyone knew it was me. There was no need for the test and anyway he didn't have a lie detector. Ironically, that in itself was a lie. This was all about control. And fear. But in that moment,

I fully believed in the lie detector lie, and I knew that I was doomed.

"It was me," I whimpered. "I'm sorry. I am really sorry."

A warped smile played around his mouth as he hauled me into the bedroom, flipped me over his knee, and pulled down my underwear. I was beaten until I begged and pleaded with him to stop.

"Waste is a sin," he said, as he stood up and smoothed a small crease out of his trousers. "Remember that. Don't ever be sick after meals again."

That evening, the preparations began for Sunday Service. Each child was required to have a bath, before laying out Sunday-best clothes, on the bed. It was, Mrs Stewart explained, vital to be clean and well presented in the House of the Lord.

"Cleanliness is next to Godliness, Monica," she told me.

I was called in first for the bath, and when I saw the steam rising from the water, I shrank back in alarm. The water was far too hot. I could see that even from the doorway.

"I'm not getting in that," I said, instinctively speaking up for myself, even though I knew it would be my downfall.

"You will do as you are told," she replied acidly. "This bath water is for everyone. You're in first, so you get it the hottest."

I am not sure, as I think back, whether my fear of the bath stemmed simply from the water temperature, or whether I connected it with the attack by my mother. Yet I had no choice but to step into the water even though it felt boiling. I stood, weeping and trembling, refusing to sit down, and watching as my pale white feet turned blotchy red under the water.

It was excruciating. I was lucky only that it was over and

done with very quickly because there was a queue of six other children waiting for the bath water. My entire body tingled as Mrs Stewart wrapped a towel around my shoulders.

"There," she said. "That wasn't so bad, was it?"

Before bed, our best clothes were laid out on the end of the eiderdown; I had been given a tartan skirt, white socks, and a white blouse. I loved the skirt and wished only that I had a nice pair of shoes to go with it. My long light brown hair was twisted into rags to be left in place overnight, to make ringlets the following morning. I was given two brushes to clean my shoes and warned not to mix them up.

"Listen, one is for polish, one is for shine," Mr Stewart said. "Get it wrong and you get battered. Again."

I brushed my horrible black shoes until I could see my face in them, all the while wondering if God might send down a new pair in exchange for me showing up at church. Maybe I could offer him some sort of deal. Then in my dressing gown, kneeling at the side of the bed, I was made to join my hands in what I would soon learn was a nightly Stewart ritual. I squeezed my eyes tight as Mrs Stewart recited a prayer:

> *'Now I lay me down to sleep,*
> *I pray the Lord my Soul to keep,*
> *If I should die before I wake,*
> *I pray the Lord my Soul to take.'*

I was supposed to join in, but I didn't know the prayer and I found myself distracted and rightly concerned by the idea that I might die before I awoke. Did she know something that I didn't? It sounded worryingly imminent, and I wanted to ask if there was an accident coming my way, but her eyes were closed and she seemed deep in concentration, so I said nothing. After the prayer, we ran through the names of the entire household, asking God to bless each one. And at the end of the list, Mrs Stewart sighed, and said, with a hint of weary resignation:

"And please God, make Monica into a good girl."

It felt as though that last request was just a step too far. As though even the Lord himself could not work miracles with a hopeless case like me.

* * * *

The next morning, there were more prayers over breakfast before we were ordered to get ready for church. The service, at 11am, was at the local parish church. Before we left, we were lined up in the hallway, seven children in descending height order, ready for inspection. Mr Stewart walked slowly from one child to the next, his small eyes boring through each face. The collective fear in the line bristled, spreading like static from one child to the next. Mr Stewart smacked his lips, preparing to speak, and there was a sharp, shared, intake of breath.

"Best behaviour," he said in a quiet voice, loaded with menace. "At all times."

He turned, slightly, and I was sure he was speaking directly to me, when he added, almost as an afterthought:

"What goes on in this house stays in this house."

He and Mrs Stewart were church elders and were involved with the Sunday services themselves and also the wider church community. It was explained to me that they were

63

members of The Guild and attended church meetings every week. I was beginning to realise that church was a big deal in the Stewart house.

We walked to the service, in that same rigid formation, tallest first, smallest last. It felt more like a military parade than a family outing. I was not used to such strict routine and several times, I felt my legs skipping off ahead, as though they had a mind of their own.

"Monica! Come back!" hissed Mrs Stewart, yanking me by the shoulder. "Back in line!"

In the church pew, we were, again, made to sit in height order, before a lady with a kind face came to call for the younger children to attend a Sunday school downstairs. Gratefully I hurried out of the bench without a second invitation. I couldn't wait to get away. And, as it turned out, I loved Sunday school. We sang songs and did drawings and listened to Bible stories. The teachers were friendly and fun. More than that, it was an escape from the Stewarts. It was an hour away from the oppression and the suffocation and the crippling fear of stepping out of line. I was fast learning that life with my foster parents was regimented and regulated; controlled and organised, right down to the last detail, right down to the last smack. And so the Sunday school, and even the church service itself, was a welcome break. I learned new songs, and I belted out the words with the kind of enthusiasm only a five-year-old can muster:

'God loves all the children, all the boys and all the girls!'

I wasn't quite sure I believed it; I certainly did not feel very loved myself. But I didn't dwell on the sentiment too much.

When I returned to the main service, back into the pew, and into my correct place according to height, I was just in time to see Mr Stewart taking the collection plate, overflowing with coins, up to the altar. Mrs Stewart was in the choir, ready to sing the final hymn. I was just a small child and so it did not strike me at all as odd that Mr Stewart could show off his family in church (in height order) before going home to oversee a child beaten black and blue. He was pious and sanctimonious and holier than thou right down to his fingernails. Yet behind closed doors, he bullied and beat a five-year-old girl. Again, I thought of the telephones in Uncle Jerry's flat. Again, all was not quite as it seemed.

"Mr Stewart! What a credit your children are," the vicar beamed, as we filed out, into the morning sunshine. "You're doing God's good work."

After we arrived home, Mrs Stewart cooked up a wonderful Sunday lunch, with roast potatoes and dumplings and a huge joint of beef. Even though I knew I could not chew such rich food, my mouth watered at the aromas coming from the kitchen. Yet even the smell of roast beef could not hide the stench of hypocrisy and misery that seeped from every brick in the house. I did not recognise it as such at that young age, but it emanated, like a bad odour, from the walls themselves.

"Grace!" rapped Mr Stewart, joining his hands, as the meal was served. "Let us be thankful!"

I could not for the life of me think what I had to be thankful about. But I was quickly learning to fall into line and keep my thoughts to myself.

At 6pm sharp, every Sunday evening, Mrs Stewart opened

what she called her 'Sweet Shop'. She would make trips to the local wholesale outlet and bulk buy boxes of sweets, before setting up a little stall at the end of the living room. Each child was given three or four pennies to spend, depending on how well they had behaved.

When I heard about the scheme, I was thrilled. I was used to getting sweeties as a regular bribe from my mother at home and I hadn't had any so far at the Stewart house. I was looking forward to a sugar fix. At 6pm precisely, Mr Stewart pressed a two pence piece into my palm with a thin and knowing smile.

"Spend it wisely," he instructed.

I picked out one penny chew and one half penny chew from the stall and leaned in, to hand over my money. But before I could pick up my purchases, Mrs Stewart tapped me lightly on the back of my hand.

"Not so fast, Monica," she admonished. "First of all, you need to tell me precisely how much change I owe you."

My mind boggled. I stared at the sweets. I stared at the coin in my hand. And in truth, I had no idea. I was five years old, I'd already missed out on great swathes of my education, and I could barely read or write or count. Basic arithmetic was quite simply beyond me. But, as always, I was happy to speak up and have a stab in the dark.

"One penny?" I said, with more hope than belief.

Mrs Stewart groaned dramatically, and the other children laughed.

"No sweets for you," Sharon laughed, as she plucked the coin from my hand. "All the more for us!"

That evening, I received another beating, to teach me to be better at arithmetic. The physical pain, as I lay in bed and sobbed, was not as bad as the isolation and loneliness that churned me up inside. I could not see it then, but the 'sweet shop' was nothing more than a way of setting me up to fail. It was just another excuse to hit me.

8

A Trip To Court

One morning, instead of me going to school with the others, Mrs Stewart announced that I would be going out on a trip with her and Mr Stewart instead. I was instantly pleased to have some time off school.

"We're going to court, Monica," she explained. "To decide where you're going to live, in the future. This is a very important day." My heart quickened as she spoke. I had no idea what court was, or even what the options were. But the idea that I might be able to leave the Stewarts, and maybe go back home, was one which filled me with excitement. I had missed my family so much, especially my dear Granny. I hardly dared hope that this might be the end of my nightmare here.

"I'll be a good girl," I promised.

Later we found ourselves in a small room at a family court, with a social worker sitting on one side of me, and Mrs Stewart on the other. It was explained to me, by the social worker, that my father had applied to a judge to be allowed to raise me by himself. My mother was no longer allowed unsupervised contact but would be allowed to see me when she was released back into society. That made little sense to me, but just the sound of my mother and father's names sent a flurry of expectation through me.

"We hope that the judge will say yes," smiled the social worker. "This really is the best option for you, Monica, to live with your father."

I had a sudden flashback to an arm being thrust through a glass window, to plates and dishes smashing, to shouting and swearing. I thought of all the weeks when Dad simply vanished from our lives. But I pushed all of that aside, into a messy heap at the side of my brain, and I prayed that the judge would be kind to me. I loved my father and I had missed him, and I desperately wanted to go home. I was confident I'd be allowed to see Granny and Grandpa every day too, just as I had before.

"I hope so too," I replied. "I'd like to live with my dad. But I miss my mum as well."

And it was true; I missed her dreadfully. For all her faults, she was my mother. She was all I had, and she was all I knew.

"You may need to tell a judge what you've just told me," the social worker added. "Don't be scared, you won't be on your own. I will be with you."

I didn't want to face a judge, but I was willing to do what it took to get myself home again. I crossed and uncrossed my fingers and thought about my teddies and my dollies and my shiny patent shoes. I remembered Granny's apron, and the feeling of her plump arms wrapped around me, like a big pillow. I thought of Uncle Jerry and his beloved Capri and the reassuring smell of petrol. I had missed them all so much. The social worker gathered up her papers and left the room, and we waited in silence for the decision of the court. It felt to me like such a long time before she reappeared, and, without making any eye contact with me, she motioned to Mrs Stewart to step outside. I watched, through a glass panel in the door, as they spoke, but I couldn't hear what they were saying. A few moments later, Mrs Stewart opened the door and said:

"Come on, Monica, we're going home now. You're coming back with us."

My little heart, which had been jumping around like an excited rabbit, fell like a lead weight, through my chest, right down to my feet.

"What about my dad?" I asked, in a small voice. "And what about my mum?"

The social worker touched my shoulder lightly.

"I'm afraid your father decided that this wasn't the right thing for him after all," she began. "And we can't let you go home to your mother. She's – away at the moment. So you'll be living with a foster family instead.

"Mr and Mrs Stewart have very kindly agreed to extend your stay with them."

As we walked out of the courtroom, my ghastly black shoes felt uglier and heavier than ever. I felt as though I was dragging the weight of all my problems in those shoes. And in many ways, I was. The tears spilled down my cheeks and splashed onto my skirt and my shoes.

"Come, Monica," said Mrs Stewart kindly, taking hold of my hand. "You're going to be just fine."

I looked at her hands, soft and clean, and her neatly clipped nails, and in a rush, I longed fiercely for my mother with her split and bitten fingernails, her blank eyes, her film star hair, her sour vodka breath. I longed for home.

Many years later, I would learn that my father had indeed applied for full custody and, when it was granted, he abruptly changed his mind and walked out of the court leaving me behind. In my view, that made the rejection a million times worse. He had filed an application probably because he wanted to be seen to do the right thing when in fact, he had no intention of following it through. My guess is that the application was nothing more than a gesture and a face-saving exercise. He didn't expect to be successful, and when he was, he panicked. It was cowardly and weak and, much as I loved him, I despised him for it too.

My grandparents could not take me in without agreeing to alienate their own daughter. If I had lived with them, they would have had to consent not to let my mother into their home unsupervised. And so, faced with that awful, impossible decision, pulled in two, opposing directions, they chose to help her and to try to save her. Later, as a parent myself, I would understand their dilemma and empathise with it. But as a small girl, trudging out of the courthouse in those frightful shoes, it was a very lonely place to be.

9

Punishments & Prayers

Over the next few weeks, life at the Stewart house settled into an uneasy military routine. Breakfast was 8am sharp, by which time the children were expected to have stirred the porridge, buttered the toast, brewed the tea, and have it ready and waiting on the dining table. Lunch, coming home from school, was 12.30pm, leaving again at 12.45pm to return to afternoon lessons. Homework was done immediately after school; the little ones at the dining table, the older ones in the bedrooms. The evening meal was at 5pm, preceded of course by prayers. Bedtime was 7.30pm for the younger ones, later for the others.

The routine reached a frantic crescendo on Saturday evenings when the church preparations began; bath and hair wash and shoe cleaning, and best clothes laid out in anticipation. Sunday Service at 11am was the peak point of the whole timetable, the pinnacle of the week's work. Nobody was allowed to miss church. Illness was not an excuse. I had the feeling even sudden death wouldn't cut it.

The punishments and the prayers continued, side by side, and I was regularly smacked for answering back or for swearing. Over time, I learned to keep my mouth shut and my thoughts locked away. And, as my stomach grew used to regular food and bigger meals, I managed to eat more and more. Mrs Stewart was an excellent cook, and I started to enjoy the recipes she prepared. There was always a soup to start with, maybe lentil or carrot, followed by a roast dinner or macaroni cheese or a stew. But the sentiment behind these meals stuck in my throat; I choked more on the pretence and the deceit than I did on the food itself. The other kids were constantly on their guard too, afraid of upsetting Mr Stewart, anxious not to get into trouble. Though he did not beat his own children as he did me, they were still wary of him. The house was thick with tension, and sometimes I could almost taste it.

As the weeks became months, my digestive system adapted further, and I vomited less often after meals, but it did not stop completely. It was as though my stomach had grown used to throwing stuff back out every now and again. On those occasions, Mr Stewart would line us all up in height order and go through the farcical rigmarole of questioning us, and threatening the lie-detector test, before settling on me as the likely culprit, with an unseemly smile playing on his lips.

"So, Monica, it's you again? Into the bedroom, pants down."

"I'm sorry," I wept. "I am so sorry."

But apologies made no difference. Tears made no difference. I just had to go through it. And so, I learned the hard way to complete my chores quickly and quietly, to avoid pun-

73

ishment. We were expected to keep our bedrooms tidy, to put away our clean clothes, to help with the washing and drying of pots. There was a brass letterbox and doorknob on the front door, and it was my job to polish those until they shone in the sunlight. The tasks were nothing out of the ordinary and often I quite enjoyed them. On Saturday nights, after the scalding hot bath, I was required to lay out my church clothes neatly on my bed before my prayers.

"And please God, make Monica a good girl," I whispered fervently, hoping against hope that he was listening.

And I began adding in requests of my own too:

"Oh, and please God, get rid of those awful shoes."

I kidded myself that he might one night magic them away, out of the window or up the chimney. But it never happened. I prayed, not because I was devout, but because I was scared. I was obedient not through choice, but through fear and oppression. Yet still, no matter how hard I tried to behave well, the Stewarts always seemed to find fault with me. I had not yet caught on that, as with the sweet shop, they were simply picking out ways in which to make me fail. And so, the more I tried, the more, conversely, I seemed to get into trouble. Mr Stewart never targeted his own children; the physical abuse was reserved only for foster children like me. It felt like I, as a long-term foster placement, got by far the most beatings. But perhaps the other foster children felt the same way too. I heard the screaming at night. I heard the footsteps on the stairs. We were all in our own private hell.

And much as I wanted to be good, the one area I could do nothing about was my schoolwork. I struggled academically, and every school parents' evening, every test, every assessment, was simply a prelude for a punishment. It was just my bad luck that the Stewarts had a son, Gordon, who was in the same class as me. And, in another stroke of devastating bad luck, he was incredibly clever. Each of my achievements was measured against his and I was consistently found to be wanting.

"Monica, why can't you do joined-up writing like Gordon?"

"Monica, why can't you count to 100 like Gordon?"

He was also quite the chatterbox and so anything at all that went wrong at school was reported straight back to the Stewarts.

"Oh Monica spelled her own name wrong today! Ha ha ha!"

He didn't do it with any malice; he was just a young boy himself. But Mr Stewart seized on every small morsel dropped by Gordon and made me suffer for it.

"Thick as two short planks, Monica, that's you," he said.

Homework was a particular trial. We had very simple tasks, perhaps only once a week, since we were still so young. But I found the work difficult nonetheless and one evening, stuck on a simple sum, $\frac{1}{2} + \frac{1}{2}$, I craned my neck to copy Gordon, who was scribbling away studiously at the other end of the dining table.

"Mummy! Monica is copying my work!" he yelled immediately.

Mrs Stewart marched into the room, eyes blazing in my direction.

"Monica! Copying is cheating. It is dishonest. It is a sin!"

she cried. "Just you wait until Mr Stewart gets home. Just you wait."

She peered over my shoulder at the sum.

"This is simple, really," she sighed. "Imagine if I have half an apple in one hand, and half in the other. How many apples do I have altogether?"

I thought hard.

"Two!" I announced with a smile.

There was a ripple of laughter around the table and Mrs Stewart shook her head in exasperation.

"Wait until Mr Stewart gets home," she repeated.

All evening, I watched the clock, still unable to tell the time, but knowing that each tick-tock brought my pain that bit closer. In bed, I lay awake, anxiously waiting. And waiting. At 9.30pm, the back door opened and, like a snuff film in which I was the sacrifice, it began. I listened for the heavy footsteps on the stairs, one step, and then another. Thirteen stairs in total. With each footstep, the fear grew, expanding in my chest, taking over, squeezing the breath from me. I could clearly see the panic; bright white and blinding. My mind ran wildly through possibilities, each more irrational than the last; perhaps I could hide under the quilt or throw myself from the window or make myself disappear? Maybe God would rescue me if I prayed hard enough? Perhaps my mother, my hopeless, feckless mother, would choose this moment to knock on the door and reclaim her missing daughter?

But none of those things happened. The door opened and there stood Bob Stewart, framed by the light from the hallway. With his white beard and his bushy white eyebrows, he glowed like a sinister Christmas decoration.

"You, Monica, are as thick as two short planks," he told me. "And you will get nowhere in life. Nowhere at all."

He said it in a matter-of-fact way as if he was commenting on the colour of the carpet. Yet each word burned. He sat on the bedroom chair and nodded quickly at me; a sign that it was time to climb out of my bunk. I had told myself that the waiting was the worst part but as his huge hand made contact with my bare flesh, I began to doubt myself. The pain was eviscerating. For some reason, I was determined not to cry. I suppose I didn't want to show him that he was winning. Yet it was agony. I choked back my screams and bit down on my lip until I could taste fresh blood. Every crack of his hand shattered the silence like thunder. My whole body shook in protest, in shock, yet still I would not let myself make a sound. I focussed on counting the smacks in my mind:

"Six, Seven, Eight, Nine…"

I couldn't count past fifteen. And I couldn't allow myself to think that he might continue past that either. After fourteen excruciating hits, Mrs Stewart appeared in the doorway and screeched:

"Enough, Bob! Enough!"

Mr Stewart shot me a look of pure disgust – and something else that I didn't recognise – as I pulled my nightdress down over my stinging buttocks. I was red raw.

"You are only here because of your foster mother," he said to me curtly. "If it was up to me, you'd be gone."

And with that, he left the room. My legs and bottom were so sore I could barely climb back into bed. I certainly could not lie on my back. Eventually, I must have sobbed myself to sleep, losing myself in dreams punctuated by flowery aprons and Woolworths pick and mix and Uncle Jerry and his orange Capri.

The following morning, Mrs Stewart was unusually kind, and she sang a little song, one I knew from church, as I was getting dressed. Before I left for school, she ruffled my hair and kissed the top of my head.

"We'll make a good girl out of you yet," she said fondly, as she waved me off.

And that evening, I was allowed, as a special treat, to stand on a stool and help stir a big pot on the stove as she cooked the evening meal. It was a bittersweet moment because it reminded me so much of Granny and of her kitchen with the back window ledge where I swung my legs and the smell of petrol sneaked in through the gaps in the window.

She did not refer to the atrocity the previous evening, but I knew that she was trying to comfort me, and I was grateful. She was never violent towards me. The punishments were always carried out by her husband and him alone and afterwards, they were never referred to again. And indeed, I reminded myself, it was her, most often, who brought a stop to them too. If it wasn't for her, screaming in the doorway, I told myself that Mr Stewart might just batter me to death one of these days. I was vulnerable, and I was crying out for someone to love me. And I had to believe that it might be her – because I had nobody else.

* * * *

At school, I slowly made friends, and I grew to adore my class teacher, aptly named Mrs Love. She had a tender and a gentle nature which reminded me very much of my aunts back at home. I started to enjoy school because, like Sunday school, it was an escape from the stiff rigidity of the Stewart household. And yet somehow, though I now had pals to play with, I still felt very much like the outsider. I thought often of Alice in Wonderland, after she swallowed the potion; I was the wrong size; I didn't fit in anywhere. I might as well have had 'Different' scrawled across my forehead in marker-pen or spray-painted across the back of my horrible duffle coat. Each day, as I dressed for school, I would pull on the shoes and whisper a silent curse.

"Bloody shoes," I muttered, out of earshot of Mrs Stewart. "Bloody, shitty, nasty shoes."

I blamed the shoes for making me feel different. It was their fault that I didn't fit in, that I never felt quite at ease. But even then, aged five, I think I knew I was lying to myself. It was easier to lay the blame on the shoes rather than admit that what really marked me out as different was an aching, screaming, lack of maternal love. There was a chasm inside me, deep and raw. A hole that only a mother could fill.

Each day, as I walked to school, I hunched over, and I folded in on myself that little bit further. I watched other families passing me by, children arm in arm with their mothers, laughing with their siblings, and I wondered why nobody ever asked me what was wrong. I wondered why nobody ever noticed that I was sad or withdrawn or crying.

Or that the tops of my legs were more often than not covered with an array of bruises, each colour-coded by date. By the time the yellow ones started to fade, there were new purple ones jostling to take their place. In PE surely, or perhaps at playtime, a teacher or a dinner-lady might have spotted them under my skirt? I wondered why nobody ever heard me screaming and sobbing at night; we had neighbours and we lived on a busy street. But, as far as I knew, not a single concern was ever raised. Nobody ever spoke of what was happening inside the Stewart house. The bricks themselves could have wept at the secrets they kept.

For my part, I never spoke up either. Never, despite my teachers and Sunday school teachers showing me such gentleness, did I even consider telling anyone about the cruelty and the punishments I endured.

"What goes on in the house stays in the house," Mr Stewart told me, again and again.

And that was enough. He didn't need to threaten me or specifically order me to lie. I was being slowly brainwashed and indoctrinated into his own personal cult. I was terrified of him and in awe of him. I would never have dared cross him. And anyway, I really didn't think anyone would be interested in what I had to say, let alone believe me. Bob Stewart was quite safe from me spilling my secrets and telling the truth. I knew my place, and, better still, he knew it too.

As for anyone else challenging the Stewarts, well, they were so well respected within the church and the community that it would probably have been unthinkable to speak out against them. Back in the early 70s, it was not acceptable, as it is now, to make allegations against people of good social standing. Mr and Mrs Stewart were revered and admired within the neighbourhood. Every time our height-descending line walked down the street, people would stop and murmur their appreciation of Bob and Teresa, that lovely couple who took in waifs and strays, who hoisted unwanted children out of the gutter and gave them a loving home.

Mr Stewart gave the readings in church on Sundays, and he did the collections too. Mrs Stewart sang in the choir. She helped organise church fairs, jumble sales and fundraisers. They both attended weekly Guild meetings and prayer groups and guidance sessions. Mrs Stewart had a vegetable patch and fruit trees in her back garden, and she made her own jams and chutneys, many of which she donated to charitable sales. All this – and they fostered children too! They were a remarkable family, or at least that was how it seemed. Mrs Stewart was known in particular for taking in babies, short-term, some drug-addicted at birth, some abandoned and abused. She was a saint, a miracle worker. She and her husband were the very last people open to criticism. They were beyond reproach.

And, to the outside world, except for the bruising, which was always on the buttocks, we were well looked after. We had good, home-cooked food. Our clothes were second hand, apart from the appalling footwear, but we didn't go without. We always had a warm coat and a decent school uniform. We saw the dentist and the doctor, when necessary, we attended school and we never missed church, ever. I had the suspicion that, should I die on a Saturday night as the prayer suggested, I would be wheeled into church the following morning regardless and propped up in the pew in my rightful position in the line. Church was more important than life itself. And certainly being seen at church was even more important than that.

It was unsurprising then, for a myriad of reasons, that the abuse from Mr Stewart went unchallenged and unchecked within the local community. And so to me, just a child, there seemed no way out. Most of the time, I felt so desperate and lonely. Some mornings, after a beating, as I walked to school, I felt as though I might be invisible. Cars drove on. Mothers scurried in front of me with their children. Even the birds in the trees seemed to hop and turn the other way as I went past. Nobody stopped to talk to me. Nobody cared. My eyes were blank, and my mind was numb, and I wondered if this was what it was like, to be my mother. Perhaps, I thought fretfully, I was slowly turning into her.

Just like the telephones I had played with as a child, the reality of life with the Stewarts was not at all as people imagined.

10

A Lonely Christmas

I had been with the Stewart family around five months when Christmas came around. As with all other events, the celebration was strictly regulated and managed. At the start of December, Mr Stewart's workplace threw a party for the children of all their employees and so we were invited. I had never been to such a big party, and I loved it. There was music playing and for a moment, I was transported back to my old house; to songs blaring from the record player, with Dad singing along. I could almost smell the cigarette smoke and see him patting his knee.

"Come on, Monica, sit up here with me and help me with the chorus!"

The Stewarts didn't play music, of course. It just wasn't that sort of house. As well as music at the party, there was dancing and games, and as much jelly and ice cream as we could eat. Again, this was nothing like the Stewarts. And at the end, a jolly Santa trundled into the great hall and opened a huge sack of presents. By now, all comparisons with Mr Stewart and Santa Claus had been wiped from my mind. I recognised him for the monster that he was. We stood in a long queue, waiting for a gift, and out of habit, I tagged on the end of the height-descending line behind the other Stewart children. Santa gave me a thick storybook with beautiful animations on each page. I was very pleased with it.

"Thank you," I beamed.

Twelve days before Christmas, we were permitted to start making paperchains and decorations for the living room. Six days beforehand, we were then allowed to string them across the ceilings. The Christmas tree went up and the countdown began. Despite the rules and regulations surrounding the hanging of every bauble, I was beside myself with excitement. I couldn't wait for Christmas Day. On the last day of term at school, there was a disco, which all my friends had been building up to for ages. It was the talk of the playground. But I didn't want to go. I had no party clothes and only one pair of shoes; the black clumpy ones. I was too ashamed to turn up in a frumpy second-hand outfit, when I knew my friends would all be wearing pretty dresses and sparkly shoes. Some of the girls even had jewellery and handbags.

"Please," I said to Mrs Stewart. "Please don't make me go."

"You have to go," she replied, in a voice which spelled the end of the matter.

And that was that. I didn't dare object any further. I knew too well what the consequences would be. The hall was rather dimly lit, and the disco was mercifully short, and I spent the duration hiding in the girls' toilets and cursing my blasted shoes. They got the blame for such a lot.

"Monica, come and dance!" shouted my pals, banging on the door of the toilet cubicle.

But there was no way I was putting myself – and my shoes – in the spotlight on the dancefloor.

"Feel sick," I replied. "Can't dance."

On Christmas Eve, we hung our seven stockings over the arm of a chair; all in order, in a line of oldest to youngest. The discipline did not waver, even on Christmas Eve. The next morning, we were allowed to rise at 7am and then each waited, in turn, to open their stocking. Mine of course was last and I was by now jumping up and down on the balls of my feet, bursting with festive joy. In my stocking, was an apple, an orange and a small xylophone. It wasn't much but I loved the little instrument and set about learning to play some Christmas carols. Later in the morning, we went to church, and I had a new skirt and jumper to wear for the occasion. Sadly though, there were no new shoes.

During the Christmas holidays it snowed heavily and every kid in the neighbourhood took a sledge up to the hill behind our estate. The Stewarts didn't have a sledge – or at least not one that I was allowed to borrow – and so I took a black bin bag out with me instead. At first, I was embarrassed when I saw the shiny red and yellow sledges that my friends had brought. But we soon found out that my binbag was by far the fastest, and I was quickly the most popular kid on the slope! We took it in turns, whizzing down the hill on the slippery plastic sheet, screaming at the top of our lungs, in a perfect mix of terror and delight. I loved feeling the cold numbing my face, with my hair flying out behind me; it was as though all of my problems were flying way behind me too. Those moments on the hill were pure joy. They were my chance to be a kid. Just a kid, and nothing more.

"Woohoo!" I yelled, landing in a snowy heap and a tangle of arms and legs, at the bottom of the hill. "Let's go again!"

Afterwards, because nobody was permitted to use the Stewarts' front door, I had to stand in the back porch and take off my wellingtons and my wet clothes, so as not to trail ice and snow into the tidy house.

"I don't want you over that doorstep dripping ice and mud into my hallway," Mrs Stewart said.

She brought me a towel and my nightdress, and, when I was acceptably clean and dry, I was finally let back into the house, to defrost my poor fingers and toes by the fire. It was almost worth enduring the freezing cold of the porch just to enjoy the warmth once again. I had physical warmth, at least, and I made the most of that.

In February 1974, I turned six, and the Stewarts bought me a small pack of colouring pencils. By now, I knew not to expect much. Everything was in moderation, everything was painfully understated, carefully rationed and meticulously planned.

"Perhaps now you would like to start calling us Mum and Dad?" Mrs Stewart said to me.

I stared, at once horrified and confused, and then quickly trying to wipe both tell-tale emotions from my face. Was this some sort of sick birthday prank? These people were not my parents, and they never would be. I no more wanted to call them Mum and Dad than I wanted to be beaten black and blue twice a week. Besides, I already had my own parents. I didn't want or need replacements. To me, they would always be Mr and Mrs Stewart. But I knew better than to point any of that out, and I rearranged my features into a grateful smile.

"Yes, Mum," I said uncertainly. "Thank you."

For my birthday, as with all the other kids, there was no traditional sponge cake. Instead Mrs Stewart planted seven candles in a 'clootie dumpling', a steamed fruit pudding. Everyone sang Happy Birthday, and, as I blew out my candles, and made my birthday wish, I focussed very firmly on my horrible shoes, and I wished very hard that they might vanish forever.

11

The Camping Trip

Early in the Spring, I was invited, along with the other girls, on a weekend Brownie Guide camp in the countryside. I had never slept in a tent before, and I could not wait. If nothing else, it represented two nights away from Mr Stewart and his big, horrible hands. But aside from that I was really looking forward to the camping. Before we left, I packed my bag, and of course I had no option but to wear my black shoes; the only pair I owned.

"Pack your gym pumps as well," Mrs Stewart advised. "Just in case you get your feet wet. You never know how the weather will be, especially when you're camping."

The weekend was brilliant; I loved the campfires, the games, and the expeditions into the woods. I had a sense of release and real happiness. On our journey home, on the minibus, I suddenly had a brilliant idea. I took my gym shoes out of the bag and slipped them on and carried my black shoes in my hand. The bus dropped me off, along with several other children, on the main road. It was only a short walk back to the house. And, along the way, I happened to pass a rubbish bin, mounted on a lamp post, near a bus stop. Scanning quickly around me to make sure that nobody was looking, I dumped my shoes into the bin. With a growing sense of triumph, I skipped home in my gym pumps, knowing that this time, after all the prayers, the wishes and the tears, those shoes had gone for good.

The moment she opened the back door, Mrs Stewart's eyes went laser-like to my feet.

"What happened to your school shoes?" she asked. "Did they get wet?"

I shook my head, confident of the fantastic lie I had formulated on the journey back.

"No," I replied gleefully. "A hungry cow ate my shoes at the camp. Just ate them all up."

She narrowed her eyes at me.

"Are you telling me the truth?" she asked, cocking her head to the side. "I don't think a cow would eat a pair of school shoes!"

I nodded vigorously.

"I saw it all myself. We were camping next to the field. He put his head over and just chewed them up. He was really hungry, I think."

Mrs Stewart said nothing else. And I felt really quite thrilled with myself. It was all I could do to stop a big, satisfied smile spreading across my face. The conversation turned to other matters during the evening meal, and I thought that was that. I would go with Mrs Stewart to buy new shoes the following day after school and do my best to persuade her to choose a different style. Perhaps I could say that the old style was too heavy for my feet – which was true, of course. Hopefully I could pick out a pair like the ones my friends had. I was busy helping to clear the dishes when there was a knock at the door, and I heard Hayley, one of my friends from further down the street.

"I was just passing, and I spotted them in the bin," she was telling Mrs Stewart. "I recognised they belonged to Monica. Nobody else has shoes quite like her."

I could barely hear the rest of what was said because my heart was hammering against my chest so loudly. The blood whooshed through my ears, blocking out everything else.

"Monica!" yelled Mrs Stewart, holding out my shoes, now damp and smelly, with a chocolate wrapper from the bin stuck to the underside. "Just you wait until your father gets home. Just you wait."

The beating that night was brutal. Mr Stewart seemed to get a puritanical kick out of hearing me scream and seeing me sob.

"You'll get nowhere in life," he told me, as the fourteenth blow smacked down on my backside. "Nowhere."

Poor Hayley had presumed she was doing me a favour, that my shoes were lost, not discarded, and I could never have told her what a drastic mistake she had made. She unquestionably would never have intended to get me into trouble.

Within the Stewart household though, I was fast learning that snitching on someone else would be of great benefit to me. If someone else was getting the beating, then logically, I was not. And, if I reported a wrong-doing, I was heaped with praise. It was a way of buying myself some valuable time in between my own punishments. I realised that all the other children did it and, worse, we were encouraged to do so and rewarded for it.

"Monica, you are such a good girl," Mrs Stewart told me, when I told tales on one of the other foster children. "I'll make sure she is punished when your father gets home."

I lay in bed that night, listening to her scream as Mr Stewart beat her with his bare hands. I wish I could have said I felt regret, but my overwhelming feeling was one of relief. I was only six years old, and it was survival of the fittest. We were purposely being turned against one another, divided and pitted against children in our own household. Perhaps it was another way of ensuring that the secrets of the house remained intact. We were all fighting against each other, isolated and alone. This way, we were unlikely ever to confide or trust in anyone ever again. It was a real-life version of Lord Of The Flies and it was exhausting to be a part of it. I was just as often the villain as the hero of course; the other kids reported me for mixing up the shoe polish brushes or dawdling on my way home from school or swearing under my breath. Time after time, I listened to Mr Stewart's terror-inducing speech about the lie detector, before owning up to take my beating. I felt as though I could rely on nobody and count only on myself.

It was a surprise, then, at tea one evening, to find that I had an unlikely ally. Mrs Stewart had piled my plate high with mince and tatties and I knew that I could not eat even half of it. Mr Stewart had told me in no uncertain terms that I was in for trouble if my plate was not cleaned. I had the growing impression they purposely gave me more food than I could manage, so that they could punish me. But there was little I could do about it.

"I'll finish it," I promised, knowing that my lie was simply staving off the inevitable.

Mrs Stewart got up to go to the kitchen, and Mr Stewart turned to pick up a fork he had dropped. In that moment, their son, Steven, who was sitting next to me, leaned over and spooned some of my dinner onto his plate. I took in a small breath of surprise, but I was careful not to say a word. I tried to thank him, with my eyes, and he winked in reply.

Moments later, he waited until both of his parents were distracted again before quickly taking some more of my dinner for himself.

"Thank you," I whispered later, as I was getting ready for bed, and he smiled and winked again.

In my prayers that night, I said: 'God bless Steven' with genuine feeling and gratitude. I had no idea why he was showing me such kindness but every drop of it was so gratefully received and so desperately needed.

12

Sink or Swim

In the summer of 1974, The Stewarts announced they were planning a trip to Canada. Mrs Stewart had relatives over there and the plan was that we would stay with them and also travel around the country. For me, it was a series of firsts; I had never been on holiday, I had never been abroad, I had never been on an aeroplane. It was mind-blowingly exciting. Later I would learn that my foster parents applied to social services to fund my place on the trip, but of course I didn't know that then.

"Canada! Canada! Canada!" I sang, dancing around the bedroom.

Part of our six-week trip was organised during term time and I took a letter into school to explain my absence. Before we left, Mrs Stewart explained that it was far too hot in Canada for long hair, before informing me that she was going to cut all of mine off. I clutched at my beloved ponytail in alarm.

"Please, no," I pleaded.

I loved my long hair. But her mind was made up. She took the scissors, and, with a savage chop, my precious ponytail was gone. I cried and cried. Tears of dismay and loss. This was another part of me chipped away, another aspect gone. I felt empty. Incomplete. Who was I becoming?

Like all children, my unhappiness did not last, and I was soon distracted by the plans for the flight and the holiday. I'd never even had a passport before. This was all such a treat. In Canada, we watched the Calgary Stampede, a huge outdoor Rodeo. We travelled through the Rocky Mountains, and we visited Niagara Falls. We even camped in a forest where there was rumoured to be a wild bear on the loose, which just made it all the more exhilarating.

Best of all, with Mrs Stewart's cousins joining us, there was a whole bunch of adults and kids, always busy, always having fun. There was no opportunity for Mr Stewart to beat or berate me. I rarely even spoke to him during the entire six weeks. The trip was brilliant, not because of my foster parents, but despite them. I was grateful for the holiday, but not at any cost. And even on a different continent, in a completely different culture, the Stewarts insisted that we attended church every Sunday. It was their main objective, on arriving in a new area, to seek out the church as a matter of urgency. Our whole itinerary was then fitted around the mass times.

That September, I moved up a class and one afternoon a week, we went for swimming lessons. I had not thought at all about the attack by my mother since it had happened, except perhaps for an inexplicable uneasiness at bath time, and I can only presume that my subconscious blotted it out for a while. Even when Mrs Stewart made me step into the scalding bath on Saturday nights, I did not link the ordeal directly with my mother and with that horrendous incident in a stranger's bathroom.

But at school, when the swimming lessons began, it was a different matter. That first week, we all trooped into the local leisure centre carrying our costumes and our towels. Still, I felt no particular sense of panic. And even as we trailed out of the changing rooms, chattering and shivering, I felt relatively calm. But, as I reached the poolside, I froze. In my ears, I could hear the rushing water. Her hands were around my neck, squeezing, squeezing, tighter and tighter. I must have fallen or stumbled because now the instructor was by my side, holding my elbow and leading me to a bench at the side of the pool.

"You look very pale," he was saying. "I think you should sit this week out. Have a glass of water and take some deep breaths."

I nodded, unable to really articulate what was wrong with me. The memories hit me in flashes and splotches; I was not sure when or where this had taken place – and of course I had no idea why. But I knew beyond all doubt that my mother's hands had been around my neck and that she had forced me under the running water. The knowledge itself was paralysing. The next week, we went to the pool for our lesson, but the same thing happened again. I almost passed out with fear. I had to sit out the lesson and wait in the changing rooms whilst my pals learned to swim. The instructor realised that I had a serious phobia and contacted the Stewarts to say it was not advisable for me to continue with swimming lessons. When Mr Stewart read the letter, he erupted.

"You're an embarrassment! A hopeless freak!" he yelled. "Poor Gordon is in the same class. You're showing him up. You're showing us all up!"

It was not like him to shout, and I felt the dread creeping up, from my toes, spreading across my body like a rash.

"Well, you're not getting away with it," he said eventually. "You will learn to swim if it is the last thing I do. I will teach you myself."

Saturday morning dawned and my nerves were jangling. At the swimming pool, he went in one changing cubicle, and barked at me to go in the adjacent one. The moment I saw the expanse of blue water, I felt my vision blurring. I gripped onto the metal handrail at the side of the pool, pleading with him to be allowed to go back.

"Please," I whispered. "Anything but this. Please."

Mr Stewart was stronger than me and, with his face turning from red to purple, he uncurled my fingers one by one from the safety bar and dragged me to the centre of the pool where he knew I could not stand up. Salty tears streamed down my face and sluiced into the pool water. I hoped desperately that someone would intervene, but the place was so busy with families, kids splashing and diving and having fun, that nobody took much notice of me.

"Right, now you're going to float on your back," he demanded.

He flipped me over, onto my back, and then he let me go. All at once I was thrashing about, swallowing great gulps of water, choking, screaming and retching. My head went under the surface once, twice, three times. Mr Stewart was yanking me up. I was unsure whether he was shoving me back under too. Everything was distorted. I felt sure I was going to drown. Eventually, probably fearing my screams would alert the lifeguard, he dragged me to the side of the pool.

"Get out," he ordered. "Get dressed. You are a disgrace."

He didn't speak to me at all in the changing rooms but once we were in the car, he exploded.

"You are a waste of space!" he screeched. "You embarrassed me in that pool. You embarrassed the whole family! Nothing good will ever come of you, Monica. Nothing!

"No wonder your own mother didn't want you, eh?"

That last insult broke my heart. I sobbed and sobbed, with my head in my hands. Once we got home, he leathered me with fourteen heavy slaps. But nothing hurt as much as those words. The worst part was it was true. He was right. She didn't want me. My own mother had tried to kill me.

The swimming lessons continued every Saturday morning, so that I began to dread the approach of the weekend. I'd lie awake on Friday nights consumed by anxiety, and wake on Saturdays with a dry mouth and a sinking heart. Sometimes, I was shaking so much I couldn't get myself changed and out of the cubicle. And each time, it was just the same. Mr Stewart peeled my hands from the safety bar, he dragged me to the deeper part of the pool, and then he watched me drowning. It was pure torture. And though I didn't realise it at the time, I now feel sure that he would have seen my social services notes before he agreed to foster me, and the attack by my mother, under the bath taps, was clearly outlined in the file. He would have known full well what I had been through and why I was so scared of water. And yet, despite that – or even because of that – he put me through it anyway. Even now, as an adult, I struggle to comprehend how anyone could show such cruelty.

13

Return to Hillside Crescent

One afternoon, I came home from school for my lunch, as usual. Mrs Stewart always insisted that we came home to eat lunch, that we were not allowed to stay and eat with our friends in the dining hall. I would much rather have stayed at school, but by now I knew better than to have an opinion. On this particular day, as I was eating a jam sandwich, Mrs Stewart said to me:

"Your clothes are out on the end of your bed. You're not going back to school. You're off to visit your mother this afternoon."

I almost choked on my sandwich. I was so taken aback; I didn't even reply.

"You do want to go, don't you?" she asked. "The social worker will be here to collect you soon. Hurry up!"

I scrambled down from my chair, stuffing the rest of the sandwich into my mouth as fast as I could.

"Manners!" rapped Mrs Stewart, and I returned to thank her for the meal and clear away my plate. I didn't want to do anything to jeopardise my visit home. But neither could I hide my enthusiasm. I took the stairs two at a time and bounded into my bedroom like an over-excited puppy. I was dressed and ready within a couple of minutes.

Once in the car, with the social worker, I concentrated on the houses and factories which whizzed past the windows, desperate to see a scene or a road that I recognised. It was a journey of about seven miles, and twenty minutes in the car. But even as the scenery grew a little more familiar, I still could not allow myself to visualise my mother and her stiff, lacquered hair, my Uncle Jerry and his beaming smile, and, of course, my dear, dear Granny. By thinking of them I felt I might somehow be jumping the gun and tempting fate, and I might not get to see them after all. I held my breath as we turned into Hillside Crescent; the road where my mother and my grandmother both lived. And now, at last, it was happening.

"Monica!" said my mother, as she opened the door.

It had been over a year since I'd seen her, but she looked just the same to me. She seemed quite pleased to see me too, and she gave me a quick embrace, more of a pat on the shoulder, which jangled her trademark bracelets, before stepping away.

"Where's Granny?" I asked. "Can I see her?"

My mother nodded. If she was upset by my eagerness to see my grandmother, and not her, she did not show it. For reasons I didn't understand, the social worker explained she would have to stay with me, throughout the visit. I would later learn that my mother had been charged with attempted murder, reduced to serious assault, and sentenced to 18 months in prison, following the attack in the bathroom. Now newly released, she was allowed only supervised access to me and was receiving psychiatric support. But aged, seven, I was mercifully spared those details.

"Can I look at my bedroom?" I asked shyly.

Somehow, though it was my house, I felt the need to ask. I wasn't even sure, come to think of it, that it was still my house. I wasn't convinced that I belonged anywhere. But I wanted to see if it was all the same; my old bedroom, my pale pink eiderdown, my light beige walls. At first, I crept along the passageway quietly, self-consciously, as though I was a nosy guest, overstepping the mark, poking around. But the moment I pushed open my bedroom door and spotted a brown teddy on the pillow, staring at me with one good eye, I felt a wave of belonging. I threw myself on the bed and was confused as the tears flowed down my cheeks, soaking the pillow and the teddy. It was like a dam, bursting. I'd kept all of this inside, all the longing, the heartache, the fear and the loneliness. And now at last, at last, I was home.

"Come on Monica," said my mother dully, appearing in the doorway. "Your Granny and Grandpa are waiting for us."

I leapt up and dried my eyes. The social worker agreed to wait outside; it seemed Granny was considered trustworthy enough to look after me by herself. We didn't even make it to the front door. As we walked up the path, there was Granny, running towards me, apron flapping, plump arms stretched out wide, and wider still, with love. She hugged me to her tightly and the smells of fresh cotton and boiled potatoes and face cream were a solace to my injured soul.

"Monica!" she beamed. "My, look at you. How you've grown! And still so pretty!"

She took me inside and it was like a hero's homecoming. My Grandpa was there, and all my aunts and uncles, including Uncle Jerry. There were neighbours and friends too. Everyone had brought me gifts, money, trinkets, toys.

"Tell me all about the foster family," Granny said, when the hugs and kisses had finally come to an end. "Are you happy?"

I looked at her face, creased with concern, and I knew I could not break her heart. I could not bring myself to tell her the truth. Besides, I was scared of confiding in her. Mr Stewart lurked in the back of my mind like a bogeyman. Though he was not there physically, the threat remained, and hovered, always, like a phantom, at my side.

'What goes on in this house, stays in this house.'

"Yes, it's fine," I said quietly. "They're nice. But it's not like home. I want to come home."

Granny's eyes filled with tears, and she pulled me to her again, my face sinking into her soft, pillowy bosom.

"You can come again before long," she whispered. "I promise."

All too soon, it was time to say my goodbyes. The journey back to the Stewarts was a sombre one. I had a million questions racing around my head.

When can I go back for another visit?

Why can't I live with my real family again?

Will I ever be allowed to leave the Stewarts?

But, even though the social worker chatted away, I said nothing. I clammed up, like a shell animal, in self-preservation. Perhaps I didn't want the honest answers to my questions, after all. The moment I got back, Mrs Stewart stepped in and relieved me of the armful of toys and trinkets I was carrying.

"I don't think so, Monica," she said abruptly. "Let's see what your father says about this when he gets home."

Mr Stewart was irrationally but predictably outraged.

"What makes you think you can walk in this house carrying gifts?" he demanded. "It's a total lack of respect. You walk in here, showing off! Don't forget what we have done for you! Don't forget your own mother doesn't want you! Show some gratitude!"

I didn't understand. I watched sadly as he tossed them all into the bin, one by one.

"She was given some money, too," Mrs Stewart told him.

"Well the money will be divided between the seven children here," he decided. "And I hope," – and here he peered closely at me – "that you will do the right thing and give your share to the church collection on Sunday."

But even Mr Stewart's cruelty could not dampen my joy that day. I went to bed with my heart singing. I remembered Granny's kisses and Grandpa's cuddles and they felt like a warm blanket around me. I couldn't wait to see them all again.

* * * *

In the weeks afterwards, I thought of little else but my family. It was as though, by going home, I had unboxed feelings which I'd been trying to bury. That one cathartic visit was a taste of how life could and should have been, and now, I wanted more. Most of all, I missed Granny, but I'd gathered that, from the social services point of view, my mother was the gatekeeper to my old life.

"When will I be allowed another visit to my mother?" I asked Mrs Stewart, sensing that I was on dangerous ground even to raise the matter with her.

"You can visit when your mother gets in touch with the social worker," she replied tartly. "It's nothing to do with you."

It seemed that it was everything to do with me, but I didn't dare push it further. Instead, in class, I day-dreamed of ways of getting home. I was too little to get on the bus, I had no money to do so, and I had no idea of the route involved. A taxi, of course, required money that I didn't have. Besides, I didn't know any taxi firms. I could call my mother myself or write her a letter. Except that I had no money for a phone box, no money for stamps, paper or envelopes. I wondered about running away, but I knew that was pointless. I didn't have the slightest idea where to run, and there would be a punishment from Mr Stewart, when I was inevitably caught. Each scenario I created only emphasised further the futility of my plans. Home was 20 minutes away, maybe less, in the car. It was so tantalisingly close. Yet it was so impossibly far. Hillside Crescent might as well have been on another planet. At night, I would lie awake, pull back the dark curtains behind the bunkbed and peer at the moon outside. On clear nights, it looked like a round coin, hanging in the sky, a reminder of the money Mr Stewart had taken from me.

"He's a bloody thief," I whispered to myself. "A bully and a thief."

It was eye-watering defiance, even in a noiseless whisper, but it gave me a momentary pleasure. In desperation, I closed my eyes, screwed up my fists, and prayed.

"Lift me out of this bed, God," I pleaded silently. "Lift me up, through the window, down the street, past the school. Please just make me fly for 20 minutes. It may take less time, flying, actually God. Maybe we could do it in 15 minutes. Just get me back home."

Sometimes, dream-like, I fancied I could feel myself levitating, off the top bunk, awkwardly around the door frame, and down the stairs, my arms waving gently by my sides, my legs paddling, a little like the swimming lessons Mr Stewart had tried to force on me. But this time, in the cold night air, it was easy. I would float serenely down to the bottom of the street, and with an inbuilt sat nav, I followed dual carriageways and roads until I got to Hillside Crescent.

I saw the street sign, with the letters peeling slightly and one 'l' missing completely, so real, so vividly accurate. It was definitely happening. I was here! I was home! But at that exact point, every time, I woke up with a cold jolt. I never made it as far as Granny's house, or mine. Tears of quiet frustration seeped from my eyes, and onto the pillow. Even my dreams were conspiring against me. Was nobody on my side? Week after week, I longed for my mother to make contact with the social workers. One half of me hated her for leaving it so long. Yet the other half of me loved her and missed her desperately. One day, maybe three months later, I came home for my lunch to find my clothes laid out on the end of my bed.

"The social worker is on her way," Mrs Stewart explained. "You're off to see your mother."

I ran out of the house, and into the social worker's car, on a euphoric high. I crossed and uncrossed my fingers throughout the entire journey, hoping that my family would all be there to see me. And it was just as I had imagined it, the most perfect of days. Granny and Grandpa made a big fuss of me and there were more cuddles and more kisses. Even my mother managed a smile.

"You're looking bonny, Monica," Granny told me. "I miss you, pet."

When it was time to leave, Granny presented me with a small green umbrella. Uncle Jerry gave me a necklace with my name on. The necklace was so pretty, and yet, inside, my heart was heavy. I could not tell them that these generous gifts were destined for the bin. That Mr Stewart would seize everything from me like a jailer.

On my way out, Granny's neighbour pressed fifty pence into my small hand. I wanted so much to give it back, to explain I was not allowed money or presents. But instead I mumbled a thank you and I got into the car with the social worker. Back at the Stewarts, once again, everything was taken from me. Mr Stewart acted as though I had stolen it all, as though it was my fault that my own family had given me gifts.

"You think you're so special," he sneered. "Well, Monica. You don't belong there, they don't want you. And you don't belong here. You're only under my roof because of my wife.

"You remember that."

And with that, he flipped open the bin and dropped my new umbrella and my sweet little necklace inside. I sank to the floor and sobbed. I felt like a blow-up ball, slashed with a knife, and with every last drop of air squeezed from me. I was flat, lifeless, directionless. That night, the tears kept on coming, and I cried and cried. The sounds and smells and sights of Hillside Crescent were an umbilical pull, a magnet, drawing me back home. My heart ached to go back.

My visits home were sporadic and always, to me at least, completely out of the blue. I might go five weeks without seeing my mother, and then five months. There was no pattern and no routine and that made it all the harder to take. Later I would learn that she spent time in psychiatric units, which went some way to explaining her unreliability. But there were other reasons too; the same reasons she could not care for me full-time herself. She was not a good mother, she was not fit to look after me, and I could not explain that away. After one visit, the social worker came into the house when she brought me back, and I heard her asking Mrs Stewart if she would like to adopt me.

"Monica isn't going to be able to go back to her birth family," she explained. "So if you'd like to submit an adoption application, we would support you."

In that moment, I felt a rush of alarm, followed, oddly, by a glimmer of hope. I didn't want Mrs Stewart to be my mother. And yet, I wanted someone to be my mother. More than anything, I wanted to be wanted. I hoped that she would file for adoption, simply as a sign that she cared for me. But Mrs Stewart very clearly and very definitely replied:

"Oh no, we won't be adopting Monica. Absolutely not."

It was another chip at my self-esteem, another puncture hole my fragile sense of self. I would later learn that Mr and Mrs Stewart received a generous fostering allowance, which would stop if they adopted me.

Over the Easter of 1975, when I was seven years old, I was taken home for a visit to see my family. My mother was still living at Hillside Crescent but, when I went into the bathroom, I noticed a stack of old furniture piled in my bedroom, and there were a couple of boxes on the bed. It looked as though she was using my bedroom as a storeroom.

"No room for me anymore," I muttered to myself, but I said nothing to her.

I did not dare to annoy her, to give her a reason not to request another visit after this one. I was taken to visit my grandparents and of course they, and my aunts and uncles, all had Easter eggs for me. I went back to the Stewart house carrying a full bag of Easter eggs. The social worker did not speak to me in the car, but, at the door, she said to Mrs Stewart:

"This child has been stuffing herself with chocolate Easter eggs the whole way home!"

My mouth fell open in astonishment. It was a blatant lie. I had no idea why the social worker would purposely tell fibs about me to get me into trouble. Besides, my bag of Easter Eggs was in my hand – unopened. There was no chocolate around my mouth, no tell-tale smears on my clothes. It was clearly an untruth. Mrs Stewart gave a sigh which said this was exactly what she had come to expect from me, and she snatched the carrier bag from my fingers.

"There will be no more of those for you," she said. "Just you wait until your father gets home."

That night, I endured another beating, and, as my screams rang through the house, I heard Steven's voice at the bedroom door.

"Leave her alone!" he demanded.

Mr Stewart stopped, hand mid-air, and looked at his son in shock.

"Hit me instead," Steven said. "Please leave her alone."

I did not know what to do. This was totally unexpected, unchartered territory. But, without another word, Mr Stewart flipped me off his knee, walked over to Steven, and punched him full in the face. They both walked out of the bedroom, Steven cradling his cheek, and I was left staring after them, wondering why my foster brother would speak up for me like that and endure pain on my behalf. The more I thought of it, the more I marvelled at his kindness. He had taken a punch, off his own father, to save me, an outsider, an alien. The social worker's deceit had left me hollow inside, but now I was filled with a warm feeling of reassurance. At last, I had someone on my side in this house. At last, I had someone who cared about me.

14

Steven

The other foster children came and went from the Stewart household; there was a long line of kids, both younger and older than me, who perhaps came overnight, or for a couple of weeks. Mrs Stewart seemed to like looking after babies too; she often had a new baby on her hip when I came home from school. And she seemed good with the little ones too; endlessly patient, clucking maternally as she rocked them to sleep or gave them bottles. I found it hard to match up this version of my foster mother with the one I knew; narrowed eyes, spittle flying from her lips in a threatening tone. The concepts of right and wrong were blurred and twisted in my mind and it seemed to me that Mrs Stewart sometimes belonged in both camps and other times, she belonged in neither.

I found it hard also to watch as all the other foster children, eventually, went home. Some were there for respite because they had a parent in hospital or in prison. Some were there because they had behaved badly, or because their parents had behaved badly. But the common thread spooling through them all was that they went home again. They might stay one night, or one week, or one month. But then they went home. So why not me?

"What's wrong with me?" I asked myself sadly. "What did I do wrong?"

One afternoon, two new children arrived, Janie and Julie. I soon learned that they were sisters; Janie was my age, and Julie was a year younger. Straightaway, we became pals. They were both very fair with white-blonde hair and painfully thin too, just as I had been. They were like frightened little field mice, scuttling across the carpet as soon as anyone even spoke to them. Poor Julie was traumatised at finding herself in a strange and hostile house and she cried every single day. She reminded me a little of myself, and I tried to look after her and protect her the best I could. And though I was still rewarded for telling tales, I didn't once snitch on Janie and Julie. My child's heart went out to them both and our friendships blossomed. During the long summer evenings of 1975, we played out until it was dark. There were big games of hide and seek, or we organised ball games in the street. We were not allowed our own bicycles but there were a few communal bikes in the shed that we could use, with permission. In those days, kids were allowed out in the streets until it was dark. I loved that small slice of freedom. Only outside, I felt I could breathe; really breathe.

That summer, we went on holiday in the family motor home, travelling around Wales. The kids slept together in an attached tent, and Mr and Mrs Stewart slept in the van. It was perfect for me; I was far enough away from those large hands and those beady eyes, and anyway, Mr Stewart was occupied with other things. I began to look on Janie and Julie as my own sisters, they meant so much to me.

"I'll look after you, always," I told them, but there was a nagging worry, in the back of my mind, that of course they could be plucked out of my life at any second, as everyone else was, and I might never see them again.

In Wales, as with all other trips away, we never missed Sunday service. Mr Stewart would seek out the nearest church in the same way that other tourists would look for a beach or a child-friendly restaurant. Our souls were taken care of – or at least they were seen to be taken care of – and that was all that mattered.

For Halloween that year, we were planning to meet with the other kids from our street for Trick or Treat. Janie and Julie were given an old sheet each, to dress up as ghosts. I stuffed a pillow up my front and down my back, to go as Humpty Dumpty. It was hilarious, trying to get down the stairs with such a lot of padding around me, and we were all jostling and laughing and in high spirits. I think, ordinarily, Mr Stewart would not have dreamed of allowing us to dress up or to take part in the Halloween celebrations. But it was important for him that he and his wife were seen by the local community to be good parents, and, in particular, good foster parents. It was probably through gritted teeth that they gave us old sheets and the loan of pillows, and they certainly went to no expense or effort beyond that. As I wobbled my way through the hallway, towards the back door, the other children giggled.

"You look so fat, Monica!" laughed Janie. "With such thin legs! Just like Humpty!"

Somehow, giggling myself, I squashed my way through the back door, and then through the porch. The others were ahead of me and so I tried to shut the porch door by pushing it closed with my pillowy bum. But clearly, I pushed too hard. Because in the next moment, there was the sound of glass shattering, followed by an outraged scream from indoors. I turned and saw the tiny shards glistening on the floor at my feet, and had a momentary flashback to the broken window in the flat, my mother's bleeding arm, my lonely journey in the dark to Granny and Grandpa's... I peered into the house, petrified, waiting for the inevitable fall-out.

"Monica!" shrieked Mrs Stewart. "What have you done?"

I had pushed right through a square glass panel in the door, and though my bum was saved from harm, because of the padding, the panel was irreparable. Mrs and Mrs Stewart did not of course ask if I was injured in any way but focussed solely on the door, on the damage I had done, and on the punishments which were lined up for me. That was the end of my Halloween celebrations. I was dragged upstairs, my underwear removed, and my backside beaten until I could cry no more. I was also grounded for a week which meant that I missed Bonfire night and the local firework display.

"You'll never amount to anything," Mr Stewart told me, with undisguised pleasure. "Never."

He had a knack of sucking the joy from every occasion. He was a true expert at ruining the lives of the children he professed to love.

* * * *

Every Thursday night, my foster parents went out to their weekly church meeting. Sharon had by now left home, and so Steven was left in charge of the younger kids. I looked forward to those evenings because he had been so kind and caring towards me; I would never forget the way he had slipped food from my plate onto his, or how he had taken a punch to the face on my behalf. Sometimes, when Mr Stewart was raging about my poor school marks, or reminding me how much I wasn't wanted in his home, Steven would slip me a quick wink or a secret smile. And that was enough to raise my spirits. His solidarity and his support, in a lonely world, meant so much to me. In Julie, I was beginning to understand how it might be to have a little sister of my own. And, in Steven, I was starting to see how it might be to have a big brother of my own.

One Thursday evening, at around 7.45pm, I was in bed, along with the other younger ones. I could tell that Janie, in the bottom bunk below me, was already fast asleep, but I felt wide-awake and unsettled. To occupy myself, I began singing my little song.

"In a big house in a green field
Far far away!
In a garden with my family
Far far away!"

I sang very quietly, not wanting to get into trouble. But then, I heard Steven's voice out on the landing.

"Sing it again," he said encouragingly, coming into the bedroom. "I like it."

He came to stand by the bunk bed, so that he could hear

me better, and I began to sing. I watched as he slipped his hand through the safety bar at the side of my top bunk. And then, to my confusion, I felt the blankets moving as his fingers, cold and slightly moist, slithered up my bare legs, like a snake.

"Keep singing," he said softly.

His eyes glazed as he reached the top of my legs. And suddenly I felt a sharp pain down below as he pushed his fingers inside me.

"It hurts!" I squealed.

"Ssshh," he said, more commanding now. "Keep singing!"

The pain was so awful that I could barely remember the words. I pushed the heels of my feet into the mattress, digging in against the appalling discomfort. It lasted probably only moments, but it felt like so much longer.

'In a green field…'

"Don't tell anyone," he whispered eventually, as his hand retreated back through the safety bar. "You are more of a sister to me than my own. You are very special, little Monica. I will always look after you."

And with that, he was gone. I lay in bed, with my mind whirring. I could almost have convinced myself that I had imagined it all, but the stinging between my legs was the single sharp and brutal reminder I needed.

I cried myself to sleep, with only my song for comfort.

'Far, far away…'

The next morning, I was bleary-eyed and tearful, but Steven behaved as though nothing had happened.

He was friendly and pleasant over breakfast, and he looked

me straight in the eye when he said: "Did you sleep well, Monica?"

And when Mrs Stewart complained that I had yawned without covering my mouth, he rolled his eyes behind her back, and smiled at me conspiratorially. My confusion deepened. Was he on my side or not? Was he my brother or was he a monster? I did not know whether I should love him or fear him.

That Saturday evening, after I had polished my shoes, ready for church the next day, Mr Stewart's voice bellowed up the stairs.

"In the hallway, now!" he ordered. "Everyone line up!"

We assembled, in height-descending order, quickly and quietly. It was another military inspection.

"Someone has mixed up the polish brush and the shine brush," he said. "And now, there is polish on the shine brush."

The announcement was made in a voice heavy with gravitas and grandiosity, as though this was a crime against the whole of humanity. A hush fell upon the line and the fear shot through us all, tallest to smallest, like an electric shock. Polish on the shine brush was a serious offence requiring a serious punishment. I felt sure that I remembered using both brushes correctly. I did not think that I was to blame. But I couldn't be certain. It was, after all, an easy mistake to make.

"And of course I have a lie detector test," Mr Stewart continued pompously. "So I will find the culprit, be in no doubt about that."

My bones themselves felt like they were trembling as he made his way down from Steven – the tallest – towards me, Janie and Julie.

"Well?" he asked, a salacious smile playing on his lips.

I hesitated. If I didn't take the beating, then Janie would. Or perhaps Julie. In a moment of courage, or maybe complete madness, I stepped forward and said meekly:

"I think it might be me."

Mr Stewart looked almost joyous as he dragged me across the hallway towards the stairs, ready for my 14 whacks across his knee.

"Stop!" Steven yelled suddenly. "Look, it wasn't her. It was me. Hit me instead!"

Astonished, Mr Stewart released his grip, more interested now in his son's blatant insubordination. He marched over to Steven and whacked him hard across the face. I felt the draft from the slap, and I saw the red mark, slightly raised, on his left cheek. As Mr Stewart thundered past us, Steven gave me a half-smile and a clandestine nod. I felt at once relief and horror; gratitude and disgust. I did not understand what had happened in the bunk bed, I had no words for the terror and the pain I felt at night. And though I knew nothing of grooming, I sensed, even as a small child, that the abuse was linked to the favours that Steven did for me and to the kindness he showed.

"Ok little Monica?" he whispered. "I've got your back."

The following Thursday evening, as I was singing in my bunkbed, Steven appeared once again at the door. I wanted to scream at him to go away and yet I also wanted him to listen to my song. Nobody else in the house was interested in me, after all. "Keep singing," he said softly, as he approached the side of the bunk. "Don't stop."

I tried to concentrate on the words, but my eyes flickered and caught the instance that his hand glided under the safety bar and under the covers. His fingers were icy-cold on my legs. The pain, once more, was excruciating. I looked past him, beyond his fixed eyes and his lips glistening with saliva in the almost-darkness. But the room around me seemed to fall away; I could not see the speckly carpet or the brown curtains or the white eiderdown. All I could see was Steven's face looming over me and it filled my vision until my mind was bursting with it.

"Don't tell anyone," he whispered, as he withdrew his fingers. "You know I love you; I love you like a sister."

Those words, so kind and yet so unspeakably cruel, swam around my head for hours and, indeed, for years. Perhaps this was what siblings did to each other in foster homes. Maybe this was normal, and I just had to get used to it. I wanted so much to be his sister. Yet at what cost? I wanted so much to be loved. Yet at what cost?

* * * *

From then, almost every Thursday evening, I was sexually abused by Steven. It followed the exact same pattern, week after week. I was made to sing the same song whilst it was happening and afterwards, using the same words, he would assure me that he loved me like a sister.

"You are very special to me…"

The nature of the abuse thankfully did not get any worse

but neither did it get any easier. I dreaded the pain and yet I was not scared of Steven himself because I thought he liked me, and he cared about me. I was able, almost, to separate Steven from the act itself. It has not escaped my notice, looking back, that the abuse, like everything else in the Stewart house, was controlled and regimented. Even sexual perversions were strictly organised and scheduled. For many weeks, I was unable to even work out that it was happening every Thursday. I had little concept of time or dates and I knew only that it took place on the nights that Mr and Mrs Stewart attended the church meetings. And so it was most unlikely – and Steven obviously gambled on this – that I would ever be able to articulate what was happening to me. He knew that I kept quiet about the physical abuse from his father and so he probably assumed I would do the same about the sexual abuse too. Besides, I had nobody to tell. Who would listen to a little girl like me? Nobody noticed my bruises. Nobody heard my screams. And nobody cared about the sexual abuse either.

On more than one occasion, Mr Stewart was downstairs, watching TV, on Thursdays. For some reason, he missed his church meetings on those evenings. And yet, the abuse continued, as usual. It was as though nothing could get in the way of the schedule.

"Sing the song," Steven ordered.

I didn't know whether he wanted me to sing to drown out the noise of my discomfort, or whether the song was all part of the ritual, all part of the kick for him.

One evening, before he left my bedroom, he paused and

said: "Remember not to tell anyone about this, Monica. You can't blab. You don't want me to have to do this to anyone else, do you?"

To my horror, he nodded towards the bunk below where Janie was fast asleep. Oddly, she had never woken or even stirred whilst I was being abused and to my knowledge, she knew nothing of it. The idea that, by saving myself, I might be condemning her to the same torture, was repugnant. If I'd had any thoughts of fighting back against Steven, they were now banished. In addition to my own torment, I was weighed down with the pressure and guilt of knowing that Janie's safety and innocence lay in my hands. I was seven years old, yet I was loaded with an unbearable responsibility and trapped in the most awful dilemma.

"Promise," I replied tearfully.

Day to day, Steven remained the same with me. He stepped in and took my punishments occasionally. He was kind to me too. My feelings became increasingly conflicted and troubled. I said prayers before every meal, I stood in a height-descending line of children, and I attended church every Sunday. On the outside, I trudged on, wearily, as normal. But it was almost impossible, hiding physical and mental abuse and keeping it all to myself. No wonder then, that I was mixed up and choked up and totally lost. I leaned heavily on that glimmer of hope, deep inside me, and though it flickered and it stuttered, it never went out completely.

* * * *

One afternoon, when I came home for lunch from school,

I was delighted to find my clothes all laid out on the bed. "Monica, you're going to visit your mother," Mrs Stewart said.

My heart did a little skip. I couldn't wait. I was eight years old by now, and my mother was still at Hillside Crescent, still the same as ever. I had never been allowed to sleep overnight with her or with my Granny. The visits were always just for an afternoon and with a social worker keeping check on me the entire time. But today, as we pulled up outside the house, the social worker, a short man with a worn-out expression, said to me: "I'm sure we can trust you and your mother to behave, can't we Monica? I will be back to collect you this evening."

I was delighted. Mum met me at the door, saw that I was alone, and said:

"Keep your coat on, we're going into town."

I followed her, tripping along in her wake, full of questions but saying nothing. She took me to two houses where I knew nobody, and I waited whilst she disappeared upstairs for a time. After the second house, she showed me a fist full of £5 notes and said:

"What do you fancy for tea?"

I beamed back in reply. She took me to a café and ordered a plate of chips and a coke for me, and nothing for herself. The bubbles from the drink went up my nose and made me giggle. The smell of the chips was so nostalgic, so comforting. I hadn't had chips since I was last with my mother. It felt wildly decadent, to be sitting in a café, wolfing down chips and slurping a fizzy drink. I imagined Mr Stewart's wrath,

Mrs Stewart's disapproving glare, and I giggled again. "If only they could see me now," I said to myself. "They'd go crazy."

I was busy with my chips when Mum excused herself to go to the loo, but, as I dipped the last one in ketchup, I realised she still wasn't back. I finished my drink too and waited a little longer. By now, the waitresses were wiping down the tables, the other customers had all left. It was almost closing time.

"My Mum is in the toilet," I told them. "I'll go and hurry her up."

I went into the ladies' loos and there she was, slumped on the toilet seat, with an empty bottle of vodka swinging in her hand. I said nothing, and returned to my chair, and stared at the formica tabletop for what felt like an age. Mum eventually staggered out, right past the table, as though she had forgotten all about me. I scurried after her, careful to keep my eyes down, wondering why, on this one day, she could not stay sober, just for me.

That night, in bed at the Stewart house, even as I cursed her, I was already missing her. She was many things, many dreadful, despicable things. But she was my mother. Her lifestyle was haphazard and perilous, and she was unreliable and irresponsible. She was at best negligent and at worst evil. There could not have been a greater contrast with the order and stifling control of the Stewart house. I almost felt, flitting between the two lifestyles, that I ought to cross a border or go through some sort of official checking system. I'd needed a passport to get into Canada – and Canada was not so different to Scotland. My mother's home, however, was in a different universe to the Stewart household. Trapped between the two worlds, I would much rather have taken my chances with my chaotic mother. But it was not my choice to make.

More confusing too was that these were two completely different and polarising lifestyles with no overlap at all. There was no easing of passage from one to the other. My mother never asked about the Stewarts; I am not sure she even knew their names. And Mr and Mrs Stewart referred only to my mother either to inform me of a forthcoming visit, or to taunt me that she didn't want me. They did not once use her name. They never discussed her or my father. I was expected to compartmentalise everything, just like the neatly folded clothes in my drawers, but I struggled to adjust to each environment after each trip. I did not know which world was mine, and, in the event, I belonged in neither.

Some weeks later, I was allocated another visit, and this time, after the usual hike around the dives and bedsits where Mum's dubious 'friends' lived, she also took me to see my Granny. I flung open the front door to see the familiar carpet runner on the stairs and the big vase at the top, full of feathery flowers that always tickled my legs when I ran past.

"Granny!" I yelled. "It's me!"

Grandpa came striding in the hallway with a big, reassuring, smile.

"Your Granny is in bed," he explained. "Nothing serious, don't look so worried. She can't wait to see you."

I crept into Granny's room and there she was, propped up

on pillows, with pale blue glass bottles, filled with Holy Water, on her windowsill. There was a bottle of fizzy Lucozade on the bedside table; that was her favourite drink.

"Come here," she said, her eyes twinkling as she patted the bed. She was not, I noticed, as pillowy as usual, and I could feel the outline of her bones as she wrapped her arms around me. But I was just so glad to see her. And afterwards, Grandpa kept me busy, letting me slot coins into the electric meter and watching the dial tick around. And then he lifted me onto the window ledge so that I could look out for Uncle Jerry, forever fixing his car. It was all so familiar that it broke my heart. This was where I belonged. And so why, every time, did I have to leave?

* * * *

For almost three years, every Thursday evening, Steven came into my room and sexually abused me. My only respite was two weeks in the summer when we went away on holiday, and those weeks when Steven was away himself. I grew to dread Thursdays, I feared and hated them. And yet, I did not hate him. He was the only person in the Stewart household who had shown me kindness and I could not put that aside lightly. I had asked him many times to stop. I had told him many times that it hurt. But his response was always the same:

"Just keep singing."

"I love you like a sister, little Monica."

And I did not dare complain any further, because I was frightened by his threat that he might transfer his attentions to Janie. Much as I struggled to live with being abused myself,

I could not have lived with knowing that I had damned her to the same fate.

And he was always very friendly to me; as a child, I told myself he was trying to make up for the Thursday torment. As an adult I now wonder whether it was just another stage of the grooming process. One morning, before school, he took a slice of toast from my breakfast plate after I whispered to him that I could not eat it.

"Our secret," he smiled.

And he leaned over my shoulder and helped with my homework more than once, too.

"No Monica, it's 'their' not 'there.' Don't worry, it's an easy mistake to make."

In his own way, he was trying to be kind to me. Or at least, I thought he was.

"You're my little sis," Steven reminded me. "I want to look out for you."

15

My Tenth Birthday

For my 10th birthday, in February 1978, there was a single rectangular parcel waiting for me downstairs. Excitedly, I unwrapped it, to find a copy of The Bible inside.

"Well?" said Mrs Stewart.

"Thank you," I stuttered, hugely underwhelmed. "Thank you very much."

In truth, I would much rather have had a Roald Dahl or an Enid Blyton book, but I swallowed down my disappointment and smiled. If this was my only present, then I would have to make the best of it. This whole house was built on deception and lies, after all, and I was a small part of it.

"This is the most important book you will ever own," Mrs Stewart told me, her voice syrupy and pious. "Don't you ever forget that."

Perhaps the words would not have jarred so sharply with me, had they not first been doused in hypocrisy and insincerity.

I was very keen, following my birthday, to visit my family, who I felt sure would have more enticing gifts wrapped and waiting for me. But it seemed weeks before the social services got in touch to say my mother had requested a visit. I could not wait to see everyone, especially Granny, and I hoped she had recovered from her illness by now. I wanted so much to buy her a little present; a bottle of Lucozade or a bunch of flowers. But I had no money. The Stewarts always made sure of that.

"Your mother has asked me to drop you at your Granny's house today," said the social worker, as I settled myself in the passenger seat. "She will be there waiting for you."

I grinned. The day was getting better and better. When we arrived, I dashed into the house, straight up the stairs, to Granny's bedroom. I ran in and was taken-aback to find the bed empty and neatly made. There was no encouraging bottle of Lucozade on the bedside table and the bottles of Holy Water, neatly placed in a ghostly blue line, stared back at me and gave away no clues.

"Granny?" I yelled, clattering back down the stairs. I ran into the living room, expecting to find her there. But instead, there was only my mother, sitting in a chair and looking straight ahead.

"Granny has gone," she said sadly, without turning her head. I glared at her suspiciously.

"Gone where?" I asked, but already, I felt the pressure rising inside my chest.

"She died," Mum replied. "I am sorry, Monica."

I felt my knees buckling under me and I gripped onto the back of the sofa to stop myself falling. I didn't understand. Granny was my one constant. My lighthouse in a stormy sea. She – and nobody else – was my very definition of unconditional love.

"No," I said fiercely. "No, she's not." I wasn't going to take this without a fight. I yelled at my mother and ran from the house, bubbling over with fury and disbelief.

"No! No! No!"

Mum did not follow me. If I hoped I could keep reality away through defiance and avoidance, then I was tragically wrong. I sat on the doorstep all afternoon, weeping and waiting for Granny, but she did not come. Later, Grandpa came home, and I could see, from his eyes, that it was true.

"I want Granny!" I wailed, hammering my small fists into the concrete path. "I need to see her!"

That evening, I was taken back to the Stewart house, and nobody mentioned my dear Granny again. I did not go to her funeral, nor did I have a chance to grieve or to say goodbye. The Stewarts did not once refer to her. She was just 59 years old and was, I learned later, a victim of cervical cancer. The shock of her death was so brutal and so unexpected that it stayed with me and weighed on me for years. In some way, even today, I feel shaken by her passing. I have never truly got over losing her or the manner of her loss.

Some years after Granny passed, my Grandpa fell asleep in front of the TV and died in a house fire. Some of the neighbours, including my friend Liz's father, battled the flames to try to save him but he was later pronounced dead in hospital. Another family eventually came to live in Grandpa and Granny's old house and, outwardly, life moved on. But, throughout my childhood, the embryonic connection with Hillside Crescent remained strong. For me, Granny's house would always feel like home.

****

In that summer of 1978, Steven got serious with a girlfriend. He was out with her most evenings, including on Thursdays too. He missed one week of abusing me, then another, and another. The relief was huge; so palpable that I could almost reach out and grab it. Somehow, after those first few weeks, I knew instinctively that it was finished. Without any words between us, without even a glance or a glare, I sensed that he was done with me. The physical and mental abuse from Mr Stewart continued as standard. It was at once amazing and disturbing, what a small child could normalise and endure. If nothing else, I was learning that I was resilient. That spark, deep inside my core, burned bright.

Following Granny's death, the contact with my mother tailed off dramatically and I realised that the visits, though formally requested by her, had probably always been instigated by Granny. But it mattered less, because I did not have the same desire to go home, without Granny there. Seeing the house, with new inhabitants, was a cruel reminder of her death and I did not want to face it. Instead, in my dreams, I clung to memories of her cluttered little kitchen, the tick-tick of the electric meter, the all-pervading smell of petrol from outside. I remembered the flowery apron with the strings flying out at the sides. And I longed for one last cuddle; one last kiss on the top of my head.

You are loved, Monica. Never forget it.

I never forgot her words. I recited them in bed each night. But it was one thing to remember them. It was quite another to believe in them.

The following summer, aged eleven, I was preparing to start high school. Now a little more mature and independent, I spent all of my spare time, after chores were done, playing outside with my friends. One sunny day, one of my pals, Pauline, said to me:

"I'm parched, Monica. Let's go to my house and get a quick drink."

I hesitated. I was expressly forbidden from going into other people's houses. Most definitely I was not allowed to invite any of my friends inside the Stewart house. I was not permitted sleepovers or friends for tea or even a pal popping in to share some homework. It simply was not tolerated.

"What goes on in this house, stays in this house," Mr Stewart told us.

The secrets of the house were undoubtedly safe, under his totalitarian discipline. But on this particular day, I was thirsty too, and so I nodded at Pauline and followed her. Both of her parents were home, and her mother greeted us at the door, all smiles, and asked if we fancied an ice-lolly. Her casual approach was astonishing. I didn't even know her and yet she was offering me food. That kind of ad-hoc generosity would never have happened with Mrs Stewart. But there were more surprises to come. Pauline walked into the kitchen, opened a cupboard door, and helped herself to two bags of crisps. She threw one in my direction and said:

"Cheese and onion OK?"

I eyed her mother warily, expecting a nuclear fall-out. But there was nothing. I couldn't believe how relaxed – how extravagant – this household was. And the way in which

Pauline and her parents communicated left me speechless. They were so easy with each other, so comfortable. I was so used to tension and pressure that I had grown to believe it was normal.

"Thank you, thank you, thank you," I said to Pauline's parents, and they laughed at my over-enthusiasm.

"You girls make sure you don't get sunstroke," they joked, as we went back out to play. "Come back for another drink in an hour."

I was perplexed by that short visit. The idea of Mr Stewart joking with his children was just absurd. I'd had no idea that other families were so friendly and laid-back, and yet felt so safe at the same time.

Over that summer, I went into other friends' houses, only very briefly, to use the loo perhaps or to grab a sandwich. And it was confirmed to me again and again that the Stewarts' house was strange; twisted, dysfunctional and regimented, way beyond what was acceptable. With the realisation came a bitterness, a longing, and an envy. I wanted a family like Pauline's. I wanted a mother who gave out ice-lollies and a father who made jokes. Instead I had a mother who drank, a father who vanished, and a foster father who mentally and physically abused me. The resentment festered like an open wound. I just wanted to be the same as everyone else. Was it too much to ask?

Another warm day, that same summer, we were playing hide and seek outside, and in the sunshine, we were quickly dehydrating. Some of the older Stewart children went back indoors to beg for a cold drink, and I followed.

"It's roasting outside," they complained. "May we have something to cool us down? Please?"

Mrs Stewart pursed her lips.

"Here," she said, placing a tray of ice-cubes on the kitchen counter. Each ice-cube was made from very diluted orange cordial. Painstakingly, she chipped out one cube at a time, seven in all. We were allowed one ice cube each and that was our lot.

"Off you go," she ordered, shooing us away like pests. "Take the ice cube and go outside."

Everything in that house; the beatings, the abuse, the food, was carefully planned and measured out. Right down to the ice-cubes.

16

High School

When Mrs Stewart took me shopping for my high school shoes, I knew better than to get my hopes up. Yet, as a little girl, it is impossible not to have hope, even just a flicker. And so, it was again a crushing disappointment when she picked out an ugly pair of clumpy black shoes, depressingly similar to the first ones she had chosen for me, six years earlier, and which she had bought variations of every two years. They looked uncannily similar to the plastic bricks used in life-saving lessons, which I had seen stacked by the side of the swimming pool on my fateful trips there. My eyes blurred with tears, and I looked at her and silently pleaded with her to change her mind.

"School is about learning, not about fashion," she told me brusquely.

And that was that. I was still extremely thin, and the big chunky shoes looked even more ridiculous on the end of my legs. I was dreading my first day at high school in East Kilbride. Though I had friends locally, many were either a year younger or older than me and so they were not in my academic year. Some of the kids from our street and from my primary school were off to different high schools too. The school was a 20-minute walk from the Stewart house, and it seemed a strange choice for my foster parents, since it was not a faith school. I had no idea why they had selected it and I didn't get to ask.

On my first morning, I tried to bottle up my apprehension as I got dressed into my uniform, a black shirt, a white blouse and a school tie. And of course, the shoes. I was desperately nervous and in need of a hug or at least a kind word. It was at times like this that I missed my Granny more than ever.

"Make sure you behave," was all Mrs Stewart said, as I stepped out into the late August sunshine.

In the playground, all my anxieties seemed to converge and smother me. The other girls were prettier than me, taller than me, with trendier hairstyles and nicer coats. And of course, they all had better shoes. In the main, they ignored me completely. But as I walked into class, I heard a snigger, and someone said:

"Lollipop legs!"

Throughout primary school, I'd battled for acceptance. Slowly but surely, I had made friendships and gained little scraps of confidence here and there. But high school was completely different, and I felt like I was picking my way through landmines. Even in that first lesson, I could feel that I was sinking. I was back on the outside, looking in, tapping on the glass. The pressure, each day, left a physical scar on me and I was more hunched over than ever. The stress of the schoolwork itself was bad enough. I was still lagging behind academically and I found the lessons and the homework quite perplexing. And, of course, Mr Stewart made sure that I didn't get away with anything.

One evening, I was poring over a particularly difficult set of equations in my bedroom, when I heard Gordon sauntering out of his room across the landing, and saying:

"Phew! I'm glad that homework's done. It was hard this week."

He and I were still in the same class, at high school, and so we had the same homework. I put down my pen and crept quietly, stealthily, across the landing. The boys' bedroom was empty and right there, by the side of his bed, was Gordon's school bag. He had even left it slightly open, almost as an invitation. I knew, if I was caught, I would get a beating. But I also knew I'd get a beating if I got my homework wrong. It had to be worth a shot.

But even my breathing sounded abnormally loud as I inched my way across the carpet, towards the bag. I held my breath until my lungs were hurting. Downstairs, I could hear Mrs Stewart beginning preparations for the evening meal. At one point, I thought I heard footsteps on the stairs, and I broke out in a cold sweat. But nobody came. Quickly, I grabbed the maths book and dashed back into my own bedroom. Within a couple of minutes, I had scrawled down the answers, together with the complex workings-out, and then I slipped the book back into Gordon's bag.

"Done," I sighed to myself.

That evening, over our meal, I expected to be confronted and punished, but nothing happened. Steven winked at me and sneaked an unwanted slice of gammon off my plate, and

I began to think my luck was turning. The next day, I handed in my homework, believing I had got away with it. If I had pulled off a gold bullion robbery, I could not have been more pleased. Later that week, we got our marks back, and I had just two wrong answers.

"18 on 20. Thanks Gordon," I whispered to myself.

That evening, Mr Stewart demanded an inspection of our schoolbooks. Still not smelling the danger, I handed mine over proudly. But within moments, he was bearing down on me angrily, his eyes glowing with fury.

"You copied Gordon!" he said, as he marched me upstairs, prodding me in the back from behind. "You're a liar. A dirty little liar."

I took the beating, with my mind still spinning. I had no idea how he'd found me out. Later, as I lay sobbing on my bed, Steven came to the doorway.

"Are you OK?" he asked softly.

"I don't understand how he knew," I sniffed.

"The wrong answers gave you away," Steven explained. "You had the same wrong answers and the same mistakes as Gordon in your workings out."

Steven's compassion was some solace. But I felt cursed. I was usually beaten for getting my homework wrong. But when I got it right, I was beaten as well. There was no way out of this. I didn't risk copying Gordon's work again, and instead I settled for poor marks. And each failure was punished with a regular beating. Yet what was sometimes more hurtful were the jibes that Mr Stewart casually threw my way.

"You'll never amount to anything, Monica," he told me. "Never forget that. Stupid through and through."

Another of his favourites was:

"Nearly, but not quite. The story of your life, eh?"

And the worst of all:

"You don't belong here. I don't want you here. And your own mother doesn't want you either."

I was whittled down by his cruelty, worn away like a sand-castle in the rain. Each insult, each smack, eroded my sense of self. Sometimes, I felt like a muddy puddle and nothing more.

* * * *

In addition to the schoolwork, I worried constantly about my peer group at high school. It wasn't that I was bullied, exactly. There were the odd few whispers and eyerolls, usu-ally directed at my coat and shoes. But I was not targeted or singled out in any way. In fact, quite the opposite. Nobody noticed me, nobody spoke to me. I wasn't even interesting enough to bully, I realised sadly. Perhaps Mr Stewart was right, after all.

"Nearly, but not quite. The story of your life, eh?"

At my new school, I was still made to walk home for lunch each day. It was a 40-minute round trip, giving me only around 15 minutes at home to eat, and of course leaving me no time to try to make friends at school. In some ways, it was a relief to escape the schoolyard every day. But I knew I stood no chance of settling in and getting in with the crowd if I was not even around. Some kids ate in the dining hall, but most went to a fast-food van which parked up, outside the school gates, every day. The smell of the hot-dogs and chips made my mouth water as I dawdled past, and reminded me, with a distant and painful pang, of my outings with my mother and the bags of chips late at night, by way of bribe or apology or because she was simply too drunk to make a meal herself. Yet, filtered through the prism of time and longing, they were fond memories. I missed the chips. I missed my mother too. And oh, how I missed my Granny.

"Are you getting a burger from the van?" one of my class-mates asked, as I pulled on the hideous duffle coat Mrs Stewart made me wear.

I shook my head despondently. Once again, I was being marked out as different, weird, alien.

"I have to go home for my lunch," I replied. "Sorry."

Although 'home' seemed something of a cruel misnomer to me, it was the only one I had. And, as the term progressed, those lunch-time trips became increasingly miserable. I seemed to spend so much of my time trudging to and from school. The autumn winds came and the cold knifed through me and my awful coat. I dreamed of huddling up in the school canteen with a hot dog or even a salad sandwich. But Mrs Stewart would not hear of it.

"No need to waste money on food at school when we can eat at home," she said. "The Lord provides, and we should always be grateful."

Now aged eleven, I was considered too old for Sunday school and so had to attend full service. It struck me, more than anything, as terminally boring. Some Sunday mornings, sitting in the pew, I could barely stay awake. And yet, as the months passed, I began to listen to the words of the readings – read, often, by Mr Stewart himself:

'...Everyone who believes in him will receive forgiveness of sins through his name...'

'...there shall be no more death or mourning, wailing or pain, for the old order has passed away...'

'...Love is patient, love is kind. It is not jealous, is not pompous, it is not inflated, it is not rude, it does not seek its own interests, it is not quick-tempered, it does not brood over injury, it does not rejoice over wrongdoing but rejoices with the truth. It bears all things, believes all things, hopes all things, endures all things. Love never fails...'

I knew already that this man was cruel and mean and violent. But now, as I watched him reading at the lectern, the realisation dawned on me that he was also a stinking hypocrite. In the choir, Mrs Stewart sang hymns about love and charity and kindness. Yet at home, my life was a misery. Week after week, I was mesmerised by Mr Stewart's self-congratulatory performances, and I marvelled at the façade he presented to the outside world. It was all about keeping up appearances and he did it so well. I would later wonder whether his involvement in the church was, itself, a sham; a calculated move, designed to help cover up what was going on in his home. After all, who would suspect a church elder of beating a foster child? Moreover, who would have the guts to accuse a church elder of beating a foster child? I would never know whether his faith was genuine. But I knew that the chasm between the two realities, of church and of home, was as wide as the gulf between my mother's lifestyle and his. As I sat on the church bench, I was reminded once again of the two ornamental telephones I had played with as a toddler. Nothing was quite as it seemed.

There was a saying amongst the church elders, which I'd heard repeated many times:

'If God takes you to it, he will pull you through it.'

I was sceptical about the existence of a higher deity, never mind a God who might actually help me through this mess. Yet I had no-one else to turn to, and so I just had to hope that the old adage had some truth in it.

****

Each week at mass, Mrs Stewart gave every child a penny to put in the collection plate. A great show was made of passing the plate down the height-descending line, so that each child could be seen to contribute, and everyone around us could take note and nod in approval of the Stewarts.

'So generous…so devout…so admirable…'

After the death of my grandmother, I had seen my mother only once, and so I'd had no sweets or treats in that time. And I was a typical eleven-year-old kid in many ways; I missed my sweets almost as much as I missed my mother. So, one week, as I clutched my penny in my hand, I suddenly came up with a plan.

As the collection plate came to me, I pretended to drop my penny amongst the others, even brushing my knuckle cunningly against the other coins for a convincing clinking sound effect. Nobody was taking much notice of me anyway and it was much easier than I had anticipated just to pop the penny into my own pocket.

"May the Lord forgive us our sins," boomed the minister, and I blushed a guilty shade of crimson. I felt the penny burning through the seam of my coat like a red-hot ember. The next morning, on my way to school, I called into the corner shop and bought myself a penny chew. Just the feel of it, squishy and sticky in my hand, sent a thrill right through me. I might just as well have been holding Willy Wonka's golden ticket. I chewed and chewed it until my jaws ached, savouring the sugar rush. It felt like the best thing I'd ever tasted in my entire life.

Even so, my secret gnawed away at me, and the guilt was hard to suppress. I had stolen money, worse, I had stolen the Lord's money, worse, I had stolen the Lord's money in the House of the Lord! It was a triple offence and I felt triple bad about it. In bed, at night, I prayed fervently for forgiveness.

"I really, really needed a sweet," I whispered. "I am so sorry God. I've not had a sweet for so long, you know that. Please don't get me into trouble over it. I'm a good girl, deep down. You know I am."

The week went on and, despite my misgivings, nobody mentioned the missing penny. It seemed I had gotten away with it. But it seemed also that I had reacquired a taste for sweets. And the following Sunday, when the collection plate came around once again, I kept my faithful penny in my coat pocket, and dropped nothing but fresh air onto the plate. I felt a funny mix of excitement and panic as the plate was passed to the row behind. I had pulled it off – again! I had money for a sweet – again! I hurried off to the sweet shop the next morning and treated myself to one, heavenly, chew. If it had been baked by the angels, it could not have tasted sweeter.

"Sorry, God," I mumbled sheepishly, as I swallowed the last of the sweet. "I am really sorry."

But before I'd even finished my apology, I knew I would do the exact same thing again the following Sunday. It was addictive, just like the sugar. I was sorry, but not that sorry. Of course, these days, I would not dream of stealing a penny. But back then, those little penny chews, on a Monday morning, gave me the lift I needed, they put a smile on my face and a smile in my tummy. I look back not in judgement that I stole the collection money, but in sadness that I was forced into such extreme behaviour.

Perhaps it was God's way of punishing me for pinching his money for penny chews, because a few months later, I started to get a toothache and eventually, with the side of my face swelling, Mrs Stewart agreed to take me to the dentist. I had gas and air and my tooth was taken out, and then, because it was lunchtime, she drove me back home for a snack. But in the car, I started to feel sick and dizzy. I couldn't eat a thing, not even soup.

"Well, you're going back to school, so don't think you can try that with me," Mrs Stewart said firmly.

I was made to walk to school for the afternoon lessons, even though I could barely see straight. And, once I arrived, a teacher sent me directly to the school nurse who called my foster mother. I was sitting right next to the nurse, with a cold cloth against my cheek, and I heard every word at the other end of the phone line.

"No I am certainly not going to collect her, she's a drama queen. She's perfectly well enough to sit in lessons and I'd thank you for sending her back there right away."

And that was it. There was a perfunctory click, and the phone went dead. It was hardly unexpected, but it added to the misery.

"Look, you can have a lie down here, in my office," the nurse said sympathetically. "Just until you get your colour back. Maybe even a little sleep?"

I managed a wonky smile of appreciation. I can't remember the school nurse, her face or her name, but that rare kindness meant a lot to me.

17

The Sick Note

Into the second year at high school, I was starting to make some close friends at last. One of my friends, Michelle Moore, would become a life-long pal. As we became teenagers, the gossip turned, inevitably, to fashion and make-up and, horror of horrors, to shoes.

"Nobody cares about your shoes, Mon," Michelle consoled me. "Nobody even notices, trust me."

But I cared. I cared a lot. The months passed, and the conversations became about boys and romance and sex. One afternoon, Mrs Stewart called me into the bathroom, and I was mortified to find her sitting on the closed toilet seat, holding a box of tampons in her lap.

Very formally, she said: "You are becoming an adult, Monica, and you will soon begin to menstruate, so you cannot let a boy touch you or you could become pregnant."

I had to stifle a smirk at this. I already knew all about sex from my school pals and I was sure that it would take more than a tap on the arm from a passing boy to get me pregnant. But I nodded gravely and kept my quips to myself.

Next, with an uptight and pained expression, she pointed in

the general direction of her nether regions with the tampon and instructed me to 'find the hole' when the time came.

"Ok," I nodded.

Little did she know, I knew full well where it was and had known since the tender age of seven. My childhood and my innocence had been ripped away from me that night, in the bunkbed, and there was no joy for me in the onset of puberty and maturity. The changes in my body brought only confusion and worry. But again, I kept my thoughts completely to myself.

"Thank you," I said politely, taking the box of tampons from her. "I am very grateful."

"You keep these out of sight," she added stiffly. "Nobody wants to see them."

Soon after, I found a bra folded neatly in my underwear drawer, next to the tampons. I felt a ripple of excitement, as any young girl would. I tried it on and giggled at the novelty. But Mrs Stewart didn't mention it at all, it was never referred to, and I followed her lead. Bizarrely, puberty was yet another taboo in the Stewart house.

One day, I came home from school for lunch, and, with the usual apathy of a teenager, I decided I could not be bothered to return for the afternoon session. Mrs Stewart was out for the day, and Mr Stewart was at work, and so I formulated a cast-iron plan to play truant without getting caught. I found some note paper and, leaning on the piano, I wrote a short letter:

'Monica has bad period cramps and must come home from school this afternoon.'

Then, using my left hand, I signed it, with a shaky: 'Bob Stewart.'

The Stewarts' piano was situated in the hallway so that all visitors would notice it and doubtless pass comment on what a musical family they were. What they didn't know – and what we certainly never dared tell them – was that we were not allowed to play it. It was all for show, and nothing more. I would have loved to take piano lessons, but the nearest I ever got was leaning on the lid to write my letter and carry out my cunning plan.

My idea was to drop the letter in at the school office and take myself off on a jaunt into town to look in the shop windows. The walk back to school did not seem so arduous that day as I thought gleefully of a whole afternoon of freedom stretching out in front of me. I was swapping double maths for a trip to Top Shop. What was not to love about that? It was all I could do to stop myself singing out loud.

As I approached the school gates, I reached into my coat pocket for the letter, but it was not there. Unfazed, I patted the other pocket. Then, I checked my blazer. Next, frantically, heart pounding, I emptied my entire schoolbag onto the pavement, shaking out the pages of each book, checking my pencil case, desperately searching for the missing note. But deep in my stomach was the creeping realisation that I would not find it.

In my mind's eye, I could clearly see my letter, with its forged signature, sitting on the piano lid. I was in two minds whether to race back and remove it – it would be better to get a late mark at school than for Mrs Stewart to find my letter – but at that moment my maths teacher appeared alongside me and said:

"Come on, I'll help you pick your stuff up. You're going to be late for class."

I had no choice but to walk into school with her, the dread sitting like a brick in my stomach. All day, I panicked. I was drenched with sweat by the time the school bell rang. By now, I knew Mrs Stewart would be home and my letter, waiting on the piano, would be in her hands. The game was up. I considered running away – but to where? I had no money, not even bus fare. And running would only prolong the agony. The beating was coming, and I had to take it. Mrs Stewart met me at the door that afternoon and said, with a weary disappointment, as though she had been expecting me to fail all along:

"Just you wait till your father gets home."

As always, I had to wait until 9.30pm for him to return from work. I lay in bed and counted the thirteen stairs as he closed in on his prey. My heartbeat thudded in time with each menacing footstep. Mr Stewart appeared at the door like the devil himself, his face set like concrete, but unable to completely wipe away all traces of a smile.

"Out of bed, Monica," he said. "You know the routine."

I knew it well. I was used to the pain. But I would never get used to the fear.

* * * *

The next day, at school, I could barely sit down in class because of my bruises. But I hid them from everyone, even my friends. Especially my friends. As always, I was desperate to blend in, to deflect attention, and, most of all, to be a part of the gang. That lunchtime, in the playground, my pals gathered together to pore over the latest edition of a women's magazine, snaffled from someone's unsuspecting mother. Feeling like an intruder, I took my place in the huddle.

"Look at this!" screeched one of my pals, holding up a page which contained a survey on sexual positions.

We laughed uproariously at this new, hilarious information, and for me, it was a welcome distraction. I giggled and gossiped like a typical teenage girl, and I honestly did not see any parallels between our playground chats and the horrors I experienced at home. I did not know – or perhaps I did not want to know – that my foster brother's motives were sexual and that I was, logically and by definition, a victim of sexual abuse. I had entombed the trauma deep in my subconscious and now, when there was possibly an opportunity to dig it out and air it, I instead pushed it deeper still. I could not, even at fourteen, articulate what had happened to me. I knew that it was wrong, and I knew that I hated it. But I also loved my foster brother and I wanted to believe that he loved me. Because if not him – then who else?

I didn't for a minute realise it was illegal, or even deeply inappropriate; my thoughts were muddied and blurred and horribly mixed up. I could not, even if my life depended on it, have shared the details of the horrific types of abuse which I had suffered in my foster family. It wasn't that I didn't want to tell anyone; the secrets hung inside me like lead weights, and I felt the physical drag of them every day. It was more that I had no idea what to tell or how to tell it or even if there was anything worthwhile to tell. I didn't know where to start, or where to end, and so, I said nothing. Besides, by sharing my secret, I would also have had to share the shame and the blame that I felt was irreversibly attached to me as a result of the abuse. I am unsure, even now, if this was a streak of self-preservation or self-destruction.

As adults, my pals have since told me that they suspected something was not right at the Stewart house. Doubtless their parents and my teachers and church elders had their own suspicions too. But nobody ever asked me if I was being ill-treated in any way. Nobody put that question to me, and, even if they had, I would probably have clammed up and retreated further into my shell. Ironically of course, there were social workers scurrying in and out of the Stewart house like cockroaches; perhaps bringing in a new foster child or taking away another. I bumped into staff from social services quite often, in passing, but they paid no attention to me unless they had come to take me to see my mother. And even then, they rarely engaged me in conversation. I did not see them as people I could trust. But what I would not know, for many years, was that certain social workers had serious concerns about my welfare.

18

Always Left Behind

In my early teenage years, the physical punishments from Mr Stewart began to slowly peter out. There was no big announcement, no official line in the sand. But gradually, I noticed he was replacing physical abuse with increasingly callous mental torture. Perhaps it was that I had reached the age of fourteen and, although only five feet tall and still very slight, I was an early developer, and I was noticeably becoming a young woman. And so maybe it was essentially a practical decision; I was getting too old and too mature to go over his knee. Obviously, I had never dared to fight back once against him, but that possibility was perhaps in the back of his mind too.

Strange as it sounds, the emotional torment was just as bad and perhaps even worse than the beatings. After every predictably poor grade at school, he would smile and his beady eyes would gleam, as though nothing could please him more than my abject failure. I dreaded taking school reports or letters home for analysis.

"You, Monica, will get nowhere in life," he told me, waving my latest D grade in front of my face. "Look at my own children, good grades every time. They'll go far. Can you explain why they do so well, and you don't?"

It was a rhetorical question, I knew that all too well, and I stared at my ugly shoes and felt the tears pricking my eyes.

"That's why you don't belong here," he finished. "Thick as two short planks. That's you."

"Sorry," I whimpered.

If my bedroom was not tidy; forensically, clinically, clean, then I was in trouble. I spent many an hour smoothing down my eiderdown so there was not a single crease left. I polished and scrubbed and hoovered until there wasn't a speck of dust anywhere. Each drawer of clothing was neatly and precisely ordered. And, as a result, over my teenage years, I developed an obsession for cleaning and tidying, which would plague me right through to adulthood. I found myself wanting, even needing, to tidy my room; unable to rest unless it was immaculate. Cleaning gave me certainty and control, in a life where I had none.

But no matter how hard I tried, how much I scoured and scrubbed, it was never enough for Mr Stewart. Now, as when I was five years old and struggling to work out my change at the 'sweet shop', I was being set up to fail. Nothing I ever did was acceptable. Mr Stewart would come into the bedroom and stalk around like a sergeant major, ignoring the other girls' beds and concentrating only on me. The inconsistency and favouritism only added to the feeling of injustice.

"You're a dirty bitch," he sneered, with a curl of his lip. "Get this place cleaned up."

I knew without doubt I could not please my foster parents.

But that did not stop me trying. There was a glint of hope inside me that meant I kept on convincing myself that next time, it might be different. Next time, I might pass the inspection. All I wanted was approval and inclusion; a kind word, a friendly nod, an arm around me. And so, I kept on leaving myself open for rejection and hurt. But that same hopeful spark kept me going too; it was a survival instinct which kept my head bobbing above water – but only just.

As I got older, I dreaded school more and more. I could not keep up academically or socially. The pressure to keep all my secrets under wraps was like trying to keep the lid on a pressure cooker. The tension and the anxiety built and built inside me and sometimes, I felt as though I might explode. I didn't know exactly what was wrong with me – but I knew there was something. There were times, part way through a geometry class or a lesson on World War Two, that I felt like screaming out loud.

"So, Monica, the date of Pearl Harbour?" asked my history teacher, knowing full well my mind was elsewhere.

I stared at him blankly. I had no room in my head for education. I had no opportunity to be a child or a teenager. That part of my life was closed off to me. The one lesson I did enjoy at school, however, was P.E. I was slim, and though I was small I had long legs, and I enjoyed athletics especially. Mrs Stewart refused to buy me a pair of running trainers, like the ones most of my pals had, and so I wore my old gym pumps instead. In the summer of 1982, at fourteen-and-a-half years old, I came first in the annual 800m race, and the sports coach was full of compliments.

"Monica, we'd love you to represent the school," she said enthusiastically. "With some training, you could really do well in the national competitions."

I nodded and smiled shyly; it was so rare for me to be complimented and I didn't really know how to react. But I already knew I would not be allowed to take part. Mr Stewart didn't like to see me being happy or having fun or doing well at anything. I most certainly was not allowed to show off a talent of any kind.

"Absolutely not," Mr Stewart scoffed, when he read the letter from the P.E. department. "You can't afford to waste time running. You need to focus on the academic side. You're way behind at school, Monica."

Another girl was instead chosen to take my place in the athletics contests, whilst I cleaned and re-cleaned my bedroom in a lonely silence.

Later that year, my disappointment thickened into despair when it was announced that Janie and Julie would be leaving the Stewart house and returning home to be with their mother. She had, apparently, sorted out her personal problems and was now in a position to care for her daughters herself. They, of course, ran around the bedroom with rampant jubilation.

"We're going home!" Janie sang. "We're going home!"

I tried hard to offer genuine congratulations, and I hope I managed to mask my own sadness.

"Bet you can't wait," I beamed. "Hope it works out."

For me, their departure was a double wound. They were my best friends in the Stewart house, and I knew I would likely never see them again. They left a gap that nobody else could fill. And I was also overwhelmed with waves of longing and bitterness and frustration.

I was glad for Janie and Julie, of course I was. Their rightful place was with their mother, just like any child. But why couldn't my mother sort herself out and take me back home? What was wrong with me? Why didn't she want me? How come everyone else seemed to leave the Stewarts for a better life? Everyone, except me.

Sometimes, I would stare at my reflection in the bathroom mirror and wonder what it was about me that marked me as an outsider. What did I do that was so dislikeable to make my own parents, my foster parents, and my foster siblings, treat me so appallingly? The shame clung to me like a dusty shroud. It never occurred to me, not once, that it might be their fault, and not mine. I blamed myself and I cursed myself and I hated myself.

After I had plastered a smile on my face and waved the girls off, in the back of the social workers' car, I locked myself in the bathroom and I sobbed. I was left behind. Again.

Nearly but not quite, Monica. Story of your life.

19

Searching for Numbness

Though I was not permitted to do anything pleasurable, or have any hobbies, at fifteen I was allowed to get a job delivering newspapers around the neighbourhood.

"It's time you learned the value of money," Mrs Stewart told me. "You need to be more self-reliant, Monica. You need to grow up."

Internally, I rolled my eyes, but I said nothing. She and Mr Stewart had never given me a penny. I knew they received a generous weekly allowance for fostering me, and very little of that was actually spent on me. And in fact, they had taken away the money which was given to me by my Granny and the rest of my family. Even so, I was keen to begin my paper round. It was an excuse for me to spend more time out of the house and it would provide me with some much-needed pocket money too. Like any teenage girl, I hankered after hair accessories and perfumes and make-up. And I idolised the same pop stars as everyone else; U2, Bananarama, and Duran Duran. I saved my paper-round wages to buy music magazines with posters inside and I learned the lyrics of every song. And on Sunday evenings, when the Top 40 countdown was announced, I was ready with a tape player and my finger hovering above the red 'record' button. It was quite an art to tape only the song itself, clipping off the DJ's voice either side of the music. At those moments, trying out new hairstyles, singing the latest songs, tacking my posters to the wall, I was one of the gang. I was a teenage girl, and nothing more. I loved those times, rare though they were. After my 15th birthday, I was allowed to go out and meet my friends in the evenings.

"Just so long as all your chores are done before you go," Mrs Stewart reminded me. "And home for 10pm sharp, and not a minute later."

It seemed to me to be a startling detour from the usual Stewart rules and regulations, and I at first wondered whether there was a catch; if I was once again being set up to get into trouble. There was something unsettling about being given permission to go out and have fun.

"Fun? Me?" I asked myself doubtfully.

But it seemed that Mrs Stewart was genuinely quite keen for me to go out each night. And so the concession brought with it a double-edged joy; the message clearly was that the Stewarts wanted me out of the house, and they did not care what happened to me. It was something I already knew but it stung to have it reinforced so coldly.

"10pm," she reminded me. "Bed for 10.15pm. Or you're grounded."

Quickly, in the evenings, the conversation amongst me and my pals turned to alcohol. In our group, as in all others, there was one girl who looked much older than her years and she was easily able to buy booze in the local off-licence. We'd pass bottles of sweet cider around in the local park, and though it was warm and slightly sour, I instantly loved the feeling it gave me inside. A few mouthfuls of cider took the edge off my anxiety; the drink calmed me down and perked me up, all at once. As if by magic, my problems seemed to blur and dissolve when I was drunk. I'd never experienced anything like it. Drinking gave me confidence too; I was suddenly chattier, wittier, prettier. I even forgot about my horrible shoes, temporarily.

I began drinking every evening and inevitably, over time, I drank more and more. Whilst my friends might get tipsy once or twice a week, for me, alcohol became a necessary crutch. Most nights I'd get blind drunk before staggering home and creeping in through the back door. More than anything, I loved the numbness. When I was out of it, I felt like a blank page, with no past, no future, and best of all, no present. It was bliss.

"Why do you have to get so hammered?" my mates asked, as I finished off another bottle. "You get wasted every night, Mon. It's not good for you!"

I shrugged. I couldn't begin to explain. Unbidden, memories of my mother swigging off the dregs of a bottle of vodka swarmed through my mind. But I shoved them out again. I was nothing like her, I told myself. Nothing.

Soon, I was spending all my money on alcohol, and I even took on a second paper round to cover my costs. For a time, I seemed to get away with it, or perhaps the Stewarts had simply lost all interest in me. One night, I was home a little earlier than usual and bumped into Mr Stewart as he arrived back from his shift at the factory. He appeared behind me on the porch, took one look at my wobbly stance, and sussed immediately that I had been drinking.

"You're grounded," he growled. "I have to say this is no surprise to me. I always knew you were going nowhere. You're an embarrassment, Monica. A total failure. It's the story of your life."

One whole week stuck at home without alcohol was a challenge for me. But by now, the owner of the local off-licence knew me well enough, and he sold me a bottle of cider the following day, without question, even though I was still in my school uniform. That night, when the house was quiet and sleeping, I swigged back big gulps of fizzy apple cider, all alone in bed. Not until my vision fogged and fuzzed and I felt the delicious nothingness enveloping me, did I finally drift into a dreamless sleep.

Another evening, after the week's punishment was up, and most of my friends were busy with their families, I walked into the town centre on my own and bought a bottle of Martini. I knocked back the lot, just wandering aimlessly around the streets. By the end of the night, I was too wasted even to stand up unaided, and it was lucky that I bumped into a couple of pals who propped me up and guided me safely home.

"You're a disgrace," Mr Stewart hissed, as I fell in through the doorway. "I never wanted you here in this house, and I was right all along."

Soon after he and Mrs Stewart announced they were going

on holiday for a week. The week passed without an issue but every night, I excused myself early and went to bed to drink myself into oblivion. When the Stewarts came home, Sally, the babysitter, called me into the living room with them.

"I think you need to know that Monica is drinking every night in bed, on her own," she told them. "It's not normal. It's not even safe. She's just a child and she has problems. She needs some help."

Visibly flustered, Mr and Mrs Stewart assured her that the matter was in hand and ushered her out of the door. I knew that they were rattled, not by my drinking itself, but by the fact that Sally had mentioned it. They didn't care one bit, in my opinion, that I was a teenage alcoholic. But they definitely didn't want word getting around. They couldn't have the neighbours knowing that their foster daughter was off the rails. The following day, I came home from school to find a social worker sitting in the front room with my foster parents.

"We've asked the social services to help you with your drinking," Mrs Stewart explained, primly pursing her lips. "We don't know what else to do with you Monica. Really, we don't know where we have gone wrong.

"We've given you everything. And this is how you repay us."

Mr Stewart nodded and gave a little sniff and my jaw dropped in astonishment. His dishonesty was breath-taking. All through my childhood when I was being abused and attacked, he had never once thought of calling a social worker. He didn't let social services know that I was battered black and blue sometimes several times a week, or that I was bullied and tormented and belittled. But now that I was drinking myself to sleep each night, as a coping mechanism, with Sally likely to share her concerns with the neighbours and, God forbid, the church-going community, it was suddenly a matter of emergency. The irony left a bitter taste in my mouth. I dropped my school bag and sank down on the sofa, opposite the social worker, with Mrs Stewart perching next to me, affecting a perplexed frown.

"Now Monica, do you have any problems?" the social worker asked. "Anything you want to discuss?"

He was a very overweight man, and I had met him years earlier when he'd taken me to visit my mother. He leaned forwards and his belly acted as a sort of shelf, holding him back. I noticed his shirt buttons straining and I thought of all the secrets waiting to burst out of this house.

"Any problems? Anything worrying you?" he repeated, with an asthmatic wheeze.

I almost laughed out loud mirthlessly at the understatement. Where to begin?

In that moment, I realised that no matter how much I kidded myself that cider offered me an escape, I was still as trapped and as suffocated as ever before. Mr Stewart was so supremely and insufferably confident in my compliance that he was happy to risk inviting a social worker into the house to grill me. He knew, with total assurance and certainty, that I could never tell him the truth. Granted, there is nothing at all to indicate that either Mr or Mrs Stewart knew about the sexual abuse by their own son. But Mr Stewart knew about the cruelty and the beatings. Because he, literally, handed them out.

"Monica?" pressed the social worker.

In the pause that followed, there was a rushing noise, like gushing water, in my ears. Was there anything bothering me? Did anything spring to mind? The social worker and Mrs Stewart waited expectantly, the silence hanging heavy and malignant between us.

"No," I said eventually, in a small, defeated voice. "Everything is OK."

I look back on my 15-year-old self and I alternately want to shake her and hug her. I should have spoken out, I should have been braver – but to what end? Would the social worker really have believed me; a mixed-up, lonely foster child, with a drink problem? Would they realistically have taken my side over Mr Stewart's? Never. I would no doubt have been labelled a liar and a fantasist and I would have been severely punished by him later for my audacity.

Besides, I was never in any real danger of spilling my secrets. I had been brought up to stay quiet and to trust nobody, not even my own parents or foster parents. I had been trained and drilled and brainwashed into keeping my own counsel. I was an expert at staying silent, and it was my specialist subject. Mr Stewart was wrong there, at least; I was good at something, after all.

20

Sweet Sixteen

In February 1984, I celebrated my sixteenth birthday. It was a Thursday and so I was at school as usual. Despite ten years of crushing disappointments and let downs, despite the warning bells clanging inside my head, I still could not help feeling excited. It was my birthday, after all. Several of my friends had already turned sixteen and had been spoiled with parties and new dresses and expensive watches. The anticipation bubbled up, into my chest, as I pulled on my school uniform. I checked my tie in the mirror with a sense of glee, knowing that soon I would be leaving school for good. I was sixteen, I was an adult, and I had everything to look forward to. Expectantly, I bounded down the stairs, into the living room, and there, wrapped and waiting on the table, was a large oblong parcel. It was by far the biggest present I'd seen in all my years at the Stewart house.

"Is it mine?" I asked, my hopes rising.

Mrs Stewart nodded.

"Happy Birthday," she smiled.

I pulled off the paper, bursting with excitement, to reveal…
a suitcase. A plain, black, plastic suitcase. My happiness was

snuffed out just as effectively as if I had been stamped upon; a small, insignificant bug underneath a giant shoe. I raised my eyes towards Mrs Stewart, and she said:

"We just thought you might like to move on, now that you're sixteen, so you will be needing a suitcase."

Even now, after years of cruelty, I was aghast; completely dumbfounded. The suitcase was my only present, and I would argue it was less of a gift and more a kick in the teeth. I had thought I was immune to their nastiness and their inhumanity, but I was wrong. I could not stomach any breakfast and later, at school, my friends clamoured around, wishing me happy birthday and wanting to know what I'd got for my all-important sweet sixteenth.

"A suitcase," I said numbly.

Their faces fell in sympathy and shock. I didn't want to tell them the truth, yet I couldn't think of a suitable white lie either. I was exhausted by all the lying, all the pretence. I felt like I was constantly holding my breath, constantly making up excuses.

"Are you OK, Mon?" Michelle asked me later.

I hunched my shoulders up and I felt myself folding and wilting, internally. I felt like I was five years old again.

"The social services payments stop when I turn sixteen," I told her. "They won't get any money for me now. So she wants me out. And she's got a pretty harsh way of letting me know."

Over the years, the question of adoption had been raised now and again by social workers, but Mrs Stewart had always dismissed it out of hand.

"That wouldn't be fair," she said to me once, vaguely, but she didn't ever explain exactly who it wouldn't be fair on.

What I did know was that by not adopting me, she had ensured that the fostering payments continued until I was sixteen. There was no birthday tea that night, no clootie dumpling and no celebration. I lay in bed and sobbed as the words of my innocent childhood song floated back into my mind:

'In a big house in a green field
'Far, far away…'

All I had ever wanted was to love and to be loved. I didn't want to be with the Stewart family any more than they wanted me there. And yet, I had nowhere to go and nobody to lean on. I thought about Granny, and I missed her so much; the pain radiated out across my chest and clutched at my heart. My breathing became sore and jagged.

Never forget you are loved.

I had to cling to that. I had to keep going, somehow. But lying there on my sixteenth birthday, and with only a suitcase to show for it, I felt more alone than ever.

Looking back, it was probably a typical teenage response to trauma, and after my sixteenth birthday I began going out and drinking even more heavily, and I bought as much alcohol, each evening, as I could afford. Following the example of all my friends, I started dating too. My boyfriend was a nice lad, my age, and with a caring nature, but I had to get myself steaming drunk before we so much as kissed.

"Am I that bad?" he asked me, in concern. "You have to get rotten before you'll let me hold your hand!"

I hadn't realised I was purposely drinking too much so that we could become close. Again, I drew no parallels with this and the abuse I had suffered. But subconsciously, I must have been dreading the intimacy.

"Lighten up," I smiled in reply. "I don't mind if you get too drunk too. I don't see the problem!"

One Saturday night, I went out to a local disco and came home, heavily intoxicated, at around 3am. Both Mr and Mrs Stewart were waiting for me in the living room; a fact which I found amusing, at that time.

"You didn't make your bed before you went out," Mrs Stewart hissed. "You know the rules. Chores first."

I nodded, still giggling, and slurred: "No problem. I'll do it now."

I stumbled into my bedroom and stripped off, down to my underwear. It seemed like a good idea to me to pull the sheet from the bed and wrap it around me, as a sort of cape. I decided to show Mrs Stewart that I was indeed in the process of making my bed and I staggered back downstairs and fell, clumsily, into the living room where they were both still sitting.

"See!" I announced.

But as I spoke, I tripped on the edge of the sheet, and it fell, leaving me exposed in the middle of the room in just my underwear. To my surprise, Mr Stewart laughed out loud. Suddenly stone-cold sober, and horribly alarmed, I grabbed the sheet and fled.

The next morning, I expected to be punished and grounded for weeks. My behaviour had been unacceptable, after all. At the very least, I was prepared for a speech from Mrs Stewart about the perils of drinking too much and staying out late, especially since I was a troubled teenage girl. But there was nothing. It was perplexing. I saw Mrs Stewart at breakfast and her face burned with silent humiliation.

She and Mr Stewart were normally very affectionate and loving towards each other, but today, they weren't speaking. I could feel the tension prickling between them. Mr Stewart looked up from his cooked breakfast, and commented:

"That was some show you put on last night."

I shrank back in disgust. Whatever this was, it was unsettling, and it felt wrong. I would rather, much rather, have taken the punishment.

* * * *

There was an atmosphere of great excitement one afternoon when I got home from school, and I found Mrs Stewart and the other children clustered around an estate agent's pamphlet.

"Look at this Monica," Gordon said. "This is our new house. We're moving!"

I glanced at the photos with little interest at first and I was determined not to be swayed by the enthusiasm. But I felt myself giving in, as I scanned the images. The house looked really posh; it was a huge step up from the current three-bedroom terrace where we lived. Over the next few weeks, we began planning and packing and the anticipation reached fever-pitch.

"I won't miss this place, that's for sure," I said to myself, as I carefully loosened the blu-tac behind my Duran Duran posters.

On the morning of the move, as I packed the rest of my stuff, I took a last look at the bedroom where I had cried so many tears. The walls felt as though they were skim-coated with my misery. I stared at the speckled carpet, the eiderdown, the small pockmarks on the wall where my posters had been. It looked, for all intents and purposes, like a typical child's bedroom. Yet behind the flowery bedspread, it was one dimensional and hollow. The whole room was a fake, nothing more than a stage set, a theatre play, a preten-sion of a happy childhood story.

"That's all it was," I murmured. "A fake."

The Stewarts had fooled most people. But they could never fool me. Moving day came and, in keeping with the routine, it ran to a strict schedule, and was remarkably organised. The new house was around ten minutes away in the car, but it was on the edge of countryside, and in a secluded spot, at the top of a country lane with a forest in the background. The house itself was detached, with a long driveway leading to the front door and a couple of acres of land. There was a cluster of outbuildings at the back, and a beautiful veranda. And at the side of the house, was a neat two-bedroom self-contained flat.

"Wow!" I whistled.

Inside the main house, there were eight large bedrooms and several bathrooms. Downstairs were huge reception rooms with open fires and wooden panelled ceilings. The kitchen dining room was open plan and absolutely cavernous. It was a stunning place. With more space, the Stewarts were able to foster more children, mainly short time respite placements. The house was lovely, there was no doubt about that. But I wondered how, exactly, it had been paid for. I'd never seen a penny of the fostering allowance, that was for sure. I had never had new clothes or toys; everything I owned came from jumble sales or Mrs Stewart's second-hand cupboard. Except, of course, for my awful shoes. There was a pile of toys in the living room which had been there since I was little. They were never replaced or updated.

In my view, this house had been their focus all along. Their new lifestyle had been funded by my misery, and others like me. Every brick of the place represented a bruise on my backside. So, all in all, the fostering had certainly paid off.

The family settled into the new house well. There was plenty of space for the younger ones to play outside. Mr and Mrs Stewart were more loving and tactile with each other than ever in their new home.

Now that I was sixteen, that level of affection, against a backdrop of eye-watering cruelty, seemed somewhat perverse. The only time I'd ever heard Mrs Stewart raise her voice, in the years of me living with them, was to scream at her husband when he was beating me. She genuinely seemed to adore him, and, in the new house, they were like honeymooners.

In truth, the entire household seemed blissfully happy. But I knew I was not part of this family. I was not welcome here. Each day, I glared at the suitcase on top of my wardrobe, and it was a cold reminder that I needed to find somewhere else to live. But where?

"Never forget you are loved," I reminded myself, but the suitcase told a different story.

Now that I was sixteen, I was free from the control of social services and able to contact my mother directly. Part of me was curious about her; I hadn't spent more than an afternoon with her since I was five years old. I didn't really feel as though I knew her very well and I decided it might be nice to spend a few days with her. Though I was aware that she had serious problems, I wanted to try to understand what lay behind them. A bigger part of me, perhaps, needed a break from the Stewart house. What, I asked myself, could be worse than the oppressive and stifling routine, the cruel and ruthless bullying from Mr Stewart, and the memories of the sexual abuse from my foster brother?

Even so, I felt a nervous thrill as I made my way to the phone box, clutching her phone number in my hand. What if she said no? She had rejected me once. She could do so again.

"Oh, hi Monica," she said, her voice as deep and husky as I remembered. "Yes, course, it would be lovely to see you."

"When?" I asked.

"Whenever," she said vaguely. "I'm not busy."

She was still at Hillside Crescent, in the old house, and I hurried home to pack my bag and speak to Mrs Stewart. She gave permission without much thought and showed little interest in my visit. She seemed to have no concerns that, at sixteen, I was going to stay with my mentally unstable and alcoholic mother who had previously tried to kill me. Her main worry, I suspected privately, was that I might not stay away as long as she'd like. Arriving at Mum's, after a long bus ride, my stomach was knotting in anxiety. And as I walked in, it was like stepping back in time, to my childhood. I could see my younger self perched on the sofa or running up and down the stairs. There was that same empty feeling inside, as if there was something missing. My mother stared blankly at me and said:

"Hello, Monica."

It was as though she'd seen me just days earlier. Despite her living alone for so long, and without my grandparents to keep an eye on her, she had not let the place go, and it was still clean and tidy. She had aged quite a lot, yet she was still an attractive woman. Gone were the high heels and all the jangling jewellery, but she looked presentable and trim in jeans and a t-shirt. She wore some make-up too, black eyeliner and a light lipstick. I noticed she was limping a little.

"What's wrong?" I asked. "Did you fall?"

"No," she replied. "I have a bad knee. I'm waiting for surgery."

Despite her limp, she was still wearing her trademark platform shoes. In many ways, she was stubborn and strong-willed, she clearly wasn't prepared to give way to her knee injury, and it saddened me that she hadn't been able to channel that spirit into becoming a better mother. I spotted an open vodka bottle on the arm of the chair and realised that little had changed, from day to day. Mum sank onto the sofa, in front of the telly, and I did the same.

"What's on?" I asked. "What are you watching?"

But she just shrugged and pulled her blanket around her. She wasn't watching anything, true to form. As evening approached, my stomach began to grumble. I knew there was no strict schedule here. Mum was still slumped on the couch with that familiar blank expression, and I realised it was up to me to prepare a meal. I opened the fridge and groaned; this was a flashback to my early years. It was practically empty except for a half-tray of eggs. The cupboards were hardly more promising. I found a couple of tins of hot dogs and a loaf of bread that was past its best. And that was it. On the gas stove there was a big stainless-steel pot filled with thick, sludgy oil.

"Mum, we've no food," I said to her.

It took a few moments for her to rouse herself. And then, half-heartedly, she flicked on the gas to heat up the pot of oil and threw in a couple of eggs. I watched, nauseated, as the fat fizzed and the yolks bobbed valiantly before vanishing under the murky surface. My delicate stomach did not thank me one bit for those two fried eggs with a hunk of dry bread. Worse still, it was the same again for breakfast the next day.

I had no money to buy food and I didn't dare to ask Mum for any. Strangely, I had never once been able to confront her about her failings as a parent. All through the years, there was an endless list of ways in which she had let me down, risked my safety, broken my heart. But I didn't say a word. Perhaps I had been so effectively conditioned and indoctrinated by the Stewarts that I no longer had the ability to face up to anyone, not even my own mother. That streak of mischief and that spirit I'd had as a child had been all but stamped out. It was there, but it was a mere flicker. I had been trained to accept what came my way without question, like a robot.

"Breakfast was nice," I lied.

Those first couple of days were difficult, primarily because I was so hungry. We survived on fried eggs and hot dogs. In the mornings, Mum sent me to the shop for a bottle of vodka, but said to me:

"You'll have to ask for tick. Tell him it's for Betty and I'll pay him at the end of the week."

It was humiliating enough, buying vodka at 10am without then explaining to the shop owner that I couldn't even pay for it. I couldn't possibly start asking if I could take a fresh loaf and a carton of milk on top of that. As I walked to the shop, I was feeling miserable and resentful and wondering why on earth I had decided to visit. Nothing had changed.

"Here's your vodka," I said sulkily, leaving it on the kitchen work surface. I looked at the thick layer of fat congealed on the pan and my stomach roiled. I was almost tempted to walk out, back to the Stewarts.

But in the evening, I found a forgotten packet of biscuits at the back of the cupboard, and Mum put on an old film, an Elvis Presley classic. We lay on the sofa together, nibbling on Digestives, snuggled up under the old red blanket, because she'd no heating. For those two hours, we were mum and daughter, and nothing more. I cherished that time; it was so precious. And, as the credits rolled, and reality made an unwelcome return, I wondered at what might have been.

Before bed, despite having a perfectly functional bathroom upstairs, Mum had a wash standing over the sink before curling up on the sofa for the night. I didn't once see her take a bath or a shower. Just as I didn't ever see her sleep in a bed. She was on the edge of society, and, in many respects, she had put herself there. She was self-marginalised, in every way, right down to her domestic routine.

On the third day, Mum got dressed and, with thickly applied make-up and high heel platform boots, she announced she was going out. I was torn between worrying about what I knew she was about to do, but relieved also that she would at least have money for food, and to pay the vodka bill, after her job was done.

"Chippy tonight," she said with a smile, and again, I felt a mix of dismay and excitement.

Later, I tucked into a salty bag of chips, which I enjoyed even more so, following my period of near starvation. Mum didn't eat, I noticed, but was content with another bottle of vodka. In many ways, staying with Mum was such fun. After the first few drinks, before she became comatose, she was sparkly and giggly, and we were like best mates. I found that I really liked her; and I was desperate to do so. Inevitably, the more she drank, the further she retreated back into herself, and she might not speak to me again for the rest of the day. But that had its advantages too. It was a break from being bullied about my poor school grades or my messy bedroom or my poor appetite. Also, with Mum, I was allowed to do what I liked and when I liked. I could lie in bed as long as I fancied; she did the same, after all, albeit on the sofa. There were no rules, there was no routine. She didn't care if I drank or smoked. She didn't even seem to notice. For me, as a teenager, it was like breaking out of a top-security prison. But despite the fact that I drank to excess in secret at the Stewart house, I didn't ever touch a drop when I was with my mother. Perhaps, subconsciously, I didn't want to be like her. Or maybe it was that I expected better of myself when I was with her. But each night, I left her to her vodka, and I was content with fizzy pop, chips and bags of sweets. I was a kid again, just like the old days. Not that Mum really paid much attention. And being allowed to do just as I liked, when I liked, only served to emphasise her failings as a mother.

There was still that gaping void inside me, that desperate yearning for any kind of mother-daughter bond. From afar, I'd watched and envied the relationship my friends had with their mothers, their shopping trips, outings to the cinema, takeaway nights at home. I wanted someone to help me with my homework and tell me off when I got drunk. I longed for someone to cuddle me if I got dumped by a boyfriend or laugh with me when I was having a bad hair day. I knew she was not that kind of mother. Absolutely not. Yet it did not stop me dreaming. Each night, she drank herself into a stupor and I'd cover her with a blanket and make sure she was breathing normally, before tiptoeing off to bed myself. In my mind's eye, I could see the ghost of my four-year-old self, baby's bottle in my hand, as I tucked her in before taking myself off to bed.

"Goodnight," I whispered.

Late one morning, during the second week of my stay, I

was woken, roughly, by my mother grabbing the shoulders of my pyjama top and hauling me out of bed.

"Ow!" I yelled, as she pinched a fingerful of skin at the same time. "What's happening?"

My mother looked wild-eyed, and I was instantly wary.

"I need you to go and borrow an iron from Helen, down the street," she told me. "I want to look smart. I'm going out."

I had a good idea why she couldn't ask for the iron herself, but I didn't dare ask. I couldn't risk refusing her, either. There was an air of instability about her this morning that was unnerving me. Quickly, I pulled on some clothes and ran down the street. When the neighbour answered, her face was vaguely familiar from my childhood.

"Sorry to ask," I began. "Could I possibly borrow your iron for five minutes?"

She sighed, in a kind way.

"Look, come in for a moment," she said. "I know who you are. You're Betty's daughter. I remember you from when you were little, and your Granny was alive."

I smiled, pleased at the rare mention of my Granny. Helen asked me to sit down and then she said:

"Listen pet, I don't want to speak out of turn. She's your mother, I get that. But I know what she did to you when you were a child. She's not to be trusted, and you're not safe there."

I bowed my head, at once humiliated yet grateful too. This woman, who I didn't even know, was more concerned for my safety than my own mother or foster mother. She gave me the loan of the iron, presumably to prevent annoying my mother, and repeated her warning at the door.

"Look after yourself," she said. "You've been through enough."

Her warning resonated. Back at the house, I made up a half-baked excuse about having to get back for school, even though I had only weeks to go until I left, and my lessons had already finished. Mum didn't pay too much heed, so it didn't really matter. I packed and left that same afternoon.

"See you soon," I said to Mum, but she was, as usual, slumped on the sofa, out of reach.

It was deeply depressing, finding myself once again under the Stewarts' roof. They were not exactly overjoyed to have me back either. I felt like a cuckoo, flitting from one home to the next and belonging nowhere.

21

Moving Out

In the summer of 1984 I left school without any qualifications; a fact which both delighted and enraged Mr Stewart.

"You'll go nowhere," he told me triumphantly. "Thick as two short planks!"

I quietly conceded, not for the first time, that he was absolutely right. College was not for me and instead I secured a YTS apprenticeship with a local hairdresser, which, it turned out, I loved. There was a real camaraderie in the salon, and I enjoyed my work too. The staff liked to gossip about the Stewarts, and I realised the family did not have quite the unblemished reputation I'd once imagined. Mr Stewart, far from being a saint, was nicknamed 'Mr Evil' by some of my clients. There were whisperings about the way the foster children were treated in his house. But my lips were clamped shut and I said nothing as I washed and conditioned head after head. Even now, given the opportunity, I could not speak out. I much preferred to listen than to talk myself. And the hair salon was the ideal place for that. The main stumbling block with my new job was the early starts; I had to be at work each morning by 8.30am, including Saturdays. I was out most nights drinking, and Friday night was always a late one for me. I struggled to get up on time for work and was often dreadfully hungover. Yet nothing could stop me going out and drinking. I needed those few hours of oblivion. But Mr and Mrs Stewart both disapproved strongly of my social life and sometimes the earache I got for a night out hardly seemed worth it. It felt like fate then, when a social worker called me soon after, to say that she knew of a council rental which might suit me. It was a flat share with three other girls, and within walking distance from the Stewart house.

"Yes," I said instantly. "I'll take it."

"You haven't even seen it yet," she laughed.

"Don't mind," I replied. "I'd like it, please. I need to get out of here."

I had no idea how I was going to pay for it. My apprenticeship wages from the hairdressers were only £27 a week. But I knew I had to get out of the Stewart house – whatever the cost. Mrs Stewart showed little emotion when I told her I was planning to move out. Perhaps a small part of me hoped she might crumple and beg me to stay, but there was nothing of the sort. She didn't ask how I was going to manage, and she certainly didn't offer me assistance or support of any kind.

As the date drew nearer, I realised I didn't even have anyone to help me carry my things. I didn't want to rely on social services; at seventeen, I was no longer their responsibility, and it wasn't as if I had a good relationship with any of the staff there. But I had no other choice.

A social worker helped me to fill out a form for an emergency loan, to cover the basics I'd need. She explained my rent would be paid, because of my low wage, but that I'd have to fund everything else myself. It was daunting but thrilling at the same time.

"My own place," I said to myself softly. "At last."

On my final night at the Stewart house, I lay in bed, wide awake, my mind a mix of trepidation and anticipation. The future was an unknown path, but whatever lay ahead had to be better than what had gone before.

On moving day, I lugged my hateful black suitcase downstairs along with a couple of carrier bags of clothes and knick-knacks. I had very little to show for my seventeen years. Heaviest of all my luggage were the secrets I carried inside me, clunky, unwieldy, and dragging me down.

"Goodbye, Monica," said Mrs Stewart, very politely, as though she really didn't know me that well at all. And in many ways, of course, she didn't. I might have been a passing stranger, for all the emotion she showed. The social worker arrived to collect me, and we packed my meagre belongings into the boot. The flat was just a five-minute drive away and on the bottom floor of a three-storey block. Instantly, as I walked in through the front door, I felt it. The lightness. The freedom. The safety.

"Hi," beamed a girl with long brown hair, who looked a couple of years older than me. "I'm Danielle. The others are at work, they'll be back later.

"You're sharing with me."

She showed me inside the first of the two bedrooms and, looking at the bare mattress, it hit me, forcefully, that I had absolutely nothing. There was no duvet, no pillows, and no bedding. I had no pots and pans, no cutlery. I didn't have soap or toothpaste. But I was determined not to let anything get in the way of my good mood.

"I'll come shopping with you," Danielle offered. "I've got the afternoon off. I can help carry your bags."

By 5pm, I had a duvet and a pillow. I had a plate, a cup, a dish and a cutlery set. I'd even splashed out to get myself a big cushion. With my loan spent, and all my wages too, I was broke. But that giddy feeling of freedom was truly priceless. I had found my sanctuary.

It didn't take long for me to settle into my new home. Sure, it was a steep learning curve; I had to teach myself how to cook and to manage my money. I realised I couldn't afford to live on takeaways and ready meals and with practice, I became a dab hand at curry and Bolognese. I had to work out how to use a washing machine too and I had plenty of wash-day disasters along the way. But I also, unusually, had lots of help; the three girls, Danielle, Tracey and Jo were keen to show me the ropes. They were all nineteen and so two years older than me, sensible and settled, with full-time jobs and busy social lives. And at the weekend, they invited me to join them on a night out. But as always, when I started drinking, I didn't stop until I passed out. I woke the next morning with a familiar blurry feeling.

"Wow," Danielle smiled, bringing me a glass of water. "You know how to party! Do you always drink that much?"

I shrugged sheepishly. It had become a habit for me and one that was hard to break. I limited my alcohol during the week because I couldn't afford it. But Friday and Saturday nights, I was out drinking myself into oblivion. I was late for work, several Saturdays, and I got into trouble with my boss. I needed to stop drinking, or cut down, at the very least. Physically now, I was away from danger. But mentally, I could never escape. The abuse squatted inside my memory, refusing to budge, leaking out toxic trails, poisoning my future, as well as my past.

The weeks flew by and there was nothing from Mr and Mrs Stewart. They didn't even send me a 'New Home' card. And even though I'd always known it, deep down, the confirmation that I had been nothing more than a pay-day for them was difficult to swallow.

One weekend, my flatmates went back home to visit their families, and, aside from work on Saturday, I had no plans of my own. I felt strangely empty and left out. I had an overpowering sense of inadequacy and failure, as though it was my fault that I didn't have a family of my own.

"What about your Mum and Dad?" asked Danielle. "Don't you see them?"

I shook my head and explained I'd been living with a foster family since I was five years old.

"Well, what about your foster parents?" she asked.

I shook my head again and then hesitated.

"I mean, yes, I suppose I could go and see them," I conceded. "They don't live far away."

I was kidding myself, as well as my flat-mates, I knew that. But it was easier to agree than to admit the reasons why I should not visit them. And I needed a family. I was desperate to be normal. I was only seventeen and I wanted someone to care about me, more than I needed to confront the demons of my past. To me, being loved, or being seen to be loved, mattered more than the abuse, and perhaps that was as a result of the abuse itself. Looking back at my teenage self, I can't explain it, even to myself. But that Sunday, I found myself outside the Stewarts' front door.

"I'm back for a visit," I announced, when Mr Stewart answered. Mrs Stewart gave me a measured and understated welcome and listened politely to my description of my new flat and my flatmates. I wanted her to know how well I was doing. Oddly, perversely, I really wanted her to be proud of me.

"Are you staying for dinner?" she asked.

"Oh, yes please," I replied, and the words were a shock, even to my own ears.

I had spent many years dreading mealtimes with this family, I had endured physical abuse rather than eat this food. And yet, here I was, voluntarily joining them around the dining table. It made no sense. And yet, there, perhaps, is the explanation. Very little in my life had made sense so far. Very little had been fair, or on my terms, or for my benefit and my happiness. And so, I did not believe that I deserved a voice.

Over the next few years, I would visit the Stewarts occasionally, never for very long, and the effort was always on my part. They never once came to see me. Nor did they ever offer me any help; financial, practical, or, God forbid, emotional. There were times when I would really have appreciated some cooking tips from Mrs Stewart, or I needed advice on changing a light bulb or wiring a plug.

Instead, I had it all to figure out on my own. There were weeks when I ran short of money, and I couldn't even afford to buy food. Again, the Stewarts did not concern themselves with that. Yet still, despite the rejection, I kept on returning. Like a little lamb, rejected by its mother, I kept on going back, only to be butted away and knocked to the ground, over and over again.

22

Old Times' Sake

One morning, I arrived for work at the salon after a couple of days off, and one of the girls said:

"Your dad called in to see you yesterday."

I stopped short.

"My dad?" I repeated. "What did he want?"

I could not imagine Mr Stewart bothering to track me down to the hair salon and my first reaction was to wonder what on earth I had done wrong now.

"He left you these," she said, handing me a lovely bouquet of flowers.

Suddenly, it all made sense. There was no way on earth Mr Stewart would ever leave me as much as a dandelion, and I knew it must have been my real father who was looking for me instead. I had not seen him at all since the fateful night my mother had tried to kill me in the bathroom. He had of course later applied for custody and won it but had changed his mind that same day. I hadn't seen him at the court. I hadn't heard a thing from him since I was five, not even a letter or a card. And now, this.

"What did he say?" I asked curiously.

The girl shrugged.

"Not much. We just told him it was your day off and he left."

I knew I should feel angry with him. But really, I was anxious to see him. He was my father, after all. Some weeks later, I went to visit my mother again, and asked if she was still in touch with him.

"Yeah," she said. "I can call him if you like. Old times' sake and all that."

That evening, there was a knock at the door, and there was my father, just as I had remembered him; undeniably older, but still sartorially impeccable in a smart suit, and with that same twinkle in his blue eyes.

"Monica," he gasped, holding out his arms, as though nothing had gone wrong between us.

It felt good to be in his arms. And I didn't want to spoil the moment by asking him where he had been all these years, why he had walked out on me in the court, and why I'd never had so much as a phone call from him as I grew up. And in all honesty, I couldn't have asked him that, anyway. I was so effectively conditioned not to stand up for myself, it had reached the point where I had completely lost my sense of self.

"I looked for you everywhere, I even found out you worked at the hairdressers," he told me. "I can't believe you've got a job! My little girl, all grown up."

I beamed. It wasn't much, but he was taking an interest, which was more than anyone else did. The evening started well enough but then he and Mum cracked open a new bottle of vodka and I felt a familiar dread crawling over my skin. It wasn't long before they were bickering and sniping at one another.

"Your fault!" she hissed at him. "This mess is all your fault. You ruined my life."

I sat quietly and listened; as invisible now, aged seventeen, as I had been aged four. No wonder I'd felt like an outsider all through my childhood; my own parents didn't even notice me. The row grew heated and Dad, it seemed, was less inebriated, and more restrained, than Mum.

"This has gone far enough," he announced, standing up and draining the last of his glass. "I'm off now, Monica."

As he turned to leave, Mum grabbed the pleat at the back of his suit jacket in both her hands and ripped it right up the middle of his spine. The jacket hung from him, and it was so strange to see my usually smart father looking so dishevelled. He glared at my mother and slammed from the flat without another word.

"Well, he deserved that," my mother slurred.

I didn't see him again for many years. But oddly, or perhaps not so, I clung to what little I had, and I kept in touch with Mum. Somehow, even though she let me down continually, I was able to whitewash each humiliation from my mind. I gave my mother chance after chance after chance. One night, I was out with a couple of pals, and we found ourselves literally walking past Mum's front door on Hillside Crescent.

"Isn't that your mum's place?" my friend, Michelle, asked. "Your old house?"

I nodded. That desire came over me again, of wanting

to have a mum like all my pals, a mum I could be proud of. Perhaps if I wanted it badly enough, it might come true.

"Let's call in and see her," I said brightly, knowing I was kidding myself but ignoring the alarm bells.

Mum answered the door, and I could tell she'd been drinking. But it was evening, and me and my pals were on a night out, so it didn't seem too out of place to them. For some reason, Mum took a shine to Michelle, and steered her off into the kitchen. Then, I heard the click of the door, and they were gone. I presumed they'd stepped out, just for a moment. But when they returned, maybe ten minutes later, Michelle was ashen, and I knew instantly something was wrong.

"Your mum took me to a house in the next street and asked me if I'd sleep with a bloke in there," she whispered.

I was aghast. Michelle was trembling with shock.

"I said no, obviously," she said, with a little nervous giggle. "But I think we should get out of here."

"You go," I said grimly. "I'll follow you outside."

It was unlike me to confront my mother, but I really felt as though I couldn't let this go. This was worse than the usual humiliation or embarrassment. She had dragged me right through the mud. I was lucky that Michelle was such a close and loyal friend, and I knew that she would keep this secret between us. Even so, the shame burned through me.

"Mum, I am so ashamed that you did that," I began, in a quiet voice. "Can you imagine..."

But she didn't let me finish. She had an upstairs living room, and she marched downstairs to lock the front door and then slipped the keys in her pocket. I stood at the top of the stairs, dismayed. Now, my friends were on the other side of a locked door and there was only one way in and out of the house.

"Don't you ever talk to me like that," Mum snarled.

She didn't usually lose her temper with me, and I was taken aback.

"Look, just let me go." I said. "Please."

"If you try to leave here tonight, I'll throw you down the stairs," she shouted. "You just watch me."

I didn't want to antagonise her any further. The stairs were steep and made of stone. I knew how vicious and unhinged she could be. She had tried to kill me once, after all. What was to stop her doing it again? As Mum walked back up the stairs towards me, I ran to the living room window, which looked out over the street, and opened it. I knew my friends were waiting below.

"Michelle! Call the police!" I shouted. "She won't let me out!"

At the mention of the police, Mum stiffened and then her mood changed abruptly.

"Oh you big baby," she sniggered. "Come on. Off you go."

I was crying and shaking as she unlocked the door to release me. She was still cackling as she gave me a little shove, out onto the pavement. I sank to my knees, the tears streaming down my cheeks, as she closed the door.

1986 - 2010
WISHAW GENERAL HOSPITAL

23

Audrey

Before my eighteenth birthday, I was introduced, through my pal, Michelle, to a young man called Simon. We were part of the same crowd of close-knit friends. He had blue eyes and light brown hair, immaculately spiked with gel. His ears stuck out a little, but he was the first to laugh at that, and I fell for his sense of humour straightaway. He was just two months younger than me and had a good job as a joiner and, more than that, he could always make me smile.

"You're the perfect solution to a bad day," I told him.

Our relationship, for the first few months, was not serious. We'd meet up on nights out, to hook up or 'get a lumber' as we called it back then. But I knew he really liked me. His blue eyes lit up every time he saw me, and he was always full of wisecracks, keen to make me laugh. My life had been pitifully short of humour to date, and I loved Simon for bringing laughter into my days.

In February 1986, I celebrated my eighteenth birthday. Many of my friends had been celebrating theirs that year and I'd been to many parties and family gatherings. Each one, lovely though it was, served as a cruel reminder that my own family would be planning no such thing for me. My birthday came and went without so much as a birthday card from Mr and Mrs Stewart. I hadn't seen them for many months, but that was perhaps all the more reason they might have wanted to contact me. My mother didn't get in touch, and I hadn't heard from my father since Mum had ripped his suit that night.

On such a milestone, I couldn't help thinking of Granny and Grandpa, and my aunts and dear Uncle Jerry. I had no idea where he was now. We'd lost touch after Granny died, she had been the glue that held us together, the best she could. Now, on the eve of my most important birthday to date, I had nobody to turn to. But my faithful pals rallied round and made up for the lack of family effort.

"No way you're letting your eighteenth pass by without a party," Michelle told me firmly. "Get dressed up. I'm taking you out."

A whole bunch of my friends gathered, including Simon, to sing Happy Birthday to me on the dance floor. It was a brilliant night and nearly, very nearly, enough to let me forget that my own mother had ignored my birthday.

Soon after, my boss at the salon announced that they were closing due to bankruptcy, and as a result I'd have to find another job. I was so disappointed. I was a few months away from qualifying as a hairdresser and now, it felt as though all that time was wasted. I looked around for another apprenticeship but ended up taking cleaning jobs and pub work to pay my bills.

By now Simon and I were getting serious, and he took me

home to meet his parents, Tom and Helen. Simon had the type of family I craved, the family I'd always dreamed of. Tom was quiet and hard-working; he had a good job as a director of a company. Helen was warm and maternal and loving, and reminded me in many ways of my dear Granny. She had a part-time job in a bookies, but her main priority was her family. I understood, as we were introduced, that I was probably not her first choice of partner for her son. I'd had a chequered and troubled upbringing, and I was currently in between cleaning jobs. But Helen welcomed me into their family without any judgement at all and she and I bonded so well.

"She is more your mum than she is mine," Simon joked. "She loves you the most!"

In the summer of 1987, when I was eighteen-and-a-half years old, I fell pregnant. Though it was unplanned, we were over the moon. Simon and I applied for our own council flat, and Helen took me under her wing even more. She came to every ante-natal appointment and check-up and, as my date drew nearer, she called me every evening, to make sure I was OK. She and Tom bought us a cot and a pram. The baby was their first grandchild, and they were bursting with excitement. I couldn't properly express my gratitude and thanks; I was overwhelmed by their kindness.

But the contrast with my own family, as always, could not have been harsher. I took Simon to visit my own mother just once, and she was drunk and abusive towards him. She didn't even know I was pregnant and there seemed little point in sharing my news with her. We went together, to see Mr and Mrs Stewart, to make our big announcement. I had warned Simon that they were unlikely to show the same enthusiasm as his own parents, but even so, their reaction was upsetting.

"I'm having a baby," I said, as we were shown into the living room.

There was a beat of silence and then Mr Stewart burst out laughing.

"That's all you bloody need," he guffawed, as if my pregnancy was a great big blunder.

Mrs Stewart pursed her lips, blinded, I presumed, by the fact that I was unmarried, and, in her eyes, and the eyes of the church, I was a hopeless sinner.

"Well, you're on your own," she said stiffly.

I had always been on my own, I wanted to retort, but of course I said nothing. We nodded and left and once outside, Simon exploded with frustration.

"Who do they think they are?" he complained. "How dare they treat you like that?"

That was only the tip of the iceberg. He had no idea of the monster that lurked beneath the surface.

"Don't worry about it," I said, slipping my hand into his. "We don't need them."

Our daughter, Audrey, was born on May 2, 1988. As I held her in my arms, I felt a wave of love so powerful, so instinctive, I could have floated away on it. I wanted to gaze at her perfect little face for the rest of my life, and I knew I'd never get bored. She was everything to me. With her sea-blue eyes and the cutest little face, she was the double of her father.

"A mini-me," Simon said proudly.

Bringing her home was the proudest day of my life. That same evening, Simon pulled the plastic wrapping off a brand-new baby bath, another gift from his parents, and said:

"Shall I fill this up in the bathroom? I'll put the heating on, warm the room up for her."

I looked back at him, my lips moving but wordless. I felt my insides icing over.

"Bath?" I stuttered eventually.

Even the word itself terrified me. Through my early childhood, I'd endured those scalding baths at the Stewart house, and, as a small girl, I had focussed more on the intolerable temperature rather than the memory of my mother's attack. Mid-teens, as soon as I was allowed, I switched to taking showers instead. I hadn't had a bath ever since and didn't intend to ever do so again. And it wasn't that the bath itself bothered me particularly. It was more the prospect of putting my own child in a bath, of placing her in a vulnerable and, in my mind, dangerous position. As a child, at the mercy of my mother, I had been betrayed by her under the bath taps, in the bathroom. Now, faced with bathing my own daughter, I was rigid with terror and confusion.

"Come on, Mon," Simon prompted me. "I've got the baby towels ready. You don't want to miss the big occasion. It's her first bath."

I felt like I was in a dream as I lifted the baby bath into the main bath and switched on the taps. Simon soothed Audrey whilst I checked the water temperature with the tip of my elbow, just as the midwife had shown me.

"In you go," Simon smiled, gently lowering our daughter into the water.

He supported her head and splashed her gently.

"She loves it!" he grinned. "I can tell. Look at her little legs kicking out."

His voice sounded so far away. I could see Audrey, distantly. I knew she was safe. But blocking my eye-line was a flashback of my mother's blank face as she gripped my shoulders and forced me backwards over the side of the bath. I watched her flick on the taps, I saw her bitten fingernails, her chipped pink nail varnish. I felt the water filling my eyes and my throat. My lungs were bursting.

"I'm just going out for some air," I said abruptly, walking out of the bathroom.

Outside, I gulped in oxygen, trying to find my sense of equilibrium again. I had to get over this. I had to be strong, for Audrey's sake. I couldn't change the past. But I could certainly focus on the future.

"Right," I said, a few moments later, back in the bathroom. "I've got her Baby Grow and her scratch mittens.

"Time for bed, little one."

I held Audrey close in the soft towel and promised her silently that I would not let her down. I was determined to devote myself to this little girl and to be the best mother I could. Without doubt, I wanted to take nothing from my own childhood. Both my own mother and my foster mother were lessons only on how not to be. The Stewarts sent a small, cheap gift for Audrey but did not visit. Helen was on hand, visiting most days and always at the end of a phone.

She was wonderful. Much as I appreciated our relationship, it brought with it a debilitating sadness too. More and more, I thought of my own mother, and wished again that she could be different. And though Helen never pressed or pried, I felt that I had to make excuses, offer explanations, for my mother, as though her failings reflected in some way on me. I felt as though I dragged her everywhere with me, like a ball and chain.

Audrey was a good baby, she slept and fed well and, as the months passed, she thrived. Simon worked hard, he was a good father, and we were happy. For the first time in my life, I belonged. I had someone who needed me – and I needed them too.

Motherhood felt like it was made for me, and I loved watching Audrey grow up; her first smile, her first word, the first time she crawled. They were moments I cherished; my oxygen and my reason for being. All the more precious too, because I knew my own mother had missed out on my milestones. Day after day, she had lain under the red blanket on the sofa, hardly acknowledging my existence. Now that I was a mother myself, I swung between anger and sympathy for her. She was a hopeless parent. I had suffered immeasurably for it. Yet undeniably, so had she.

One night, soon after I turned nineteen, Simon took me out dancing, and of course Helen was only too happy to babysit.

"You don't get out much," she smiled. "I don't want you back here too early!"

I'd made a big effort, wearing my favourite strapless black

dress, with black high heels and diamante jewellery. My hair was done up in a fancy bun.

"You look beautiful," Simon smiled.

That night, in front of everyone in a packed nightclub, he proposed.

"Yes!" I yelled above the music. "Of course I'll marry you. I love you!"

24

The Wedding

Our wedding date was set for September 29, 1990, at Claremont Parish Church, East Kilbride. I would have been happier with a low-key register office ceremony; I'd had my fill of sitting in church and saying prayers that nobody ever listened to. But Simon didn't know that, and he wanted a big traditional wedding.

"Only the best for you," he smiled.

He paid for the entire day himself too. My mother could not contribute, and the Stewarts would not contribute. In the event, we didn't even ask them.

"We're not inviting them either," Simon said firmly. "They don't treat you very well."

I was happy to follow his lead; grateful that I had someone on my side. I asked Simon's dad to walk me down the aisle and the joy on his face as he accepted was at once heart-warming and heart-breaking. The night before the wedding, there was a hammering on our front door, and I heard my mother's voice outside. She was drunk and incoherently wailing abuse. Somehow, she had found out that I was getting married.

"You're not coming," Simon told her curtly. "Go away. We don't want you here."

He closed the door firmly and that was that. Again, I was so appreciative that I had someone to speak for me, to think of me. And in marrying Simon, I was joining his wider family, and that made me so happy. The sense of belonging I got from being a mother, a wife, a daughter-in-law, felt like the missing piece of a jigsaw.

* * * *

When Audrey was about two months old, I took her to meet The Stewart family. I could not justify the decision, even to myself. But my need and longing for their approval was overwhelming, and a part of me admittedly wanted to show Audrey off. I was desperate for them to admire her and love her and show her the affection they had never shown to me. Of course, now I had Simon's family and I was grateful. But their warmth and generosity only served to accentuate the lack of involvement from my own side of the family. Deep down, a part of me wanted that to change. That same spark of hope which had kept me going all through the miserable years of my childhood, now kept alive my dream that the Stewarts would one day accept me and my daughter.

"Here she is," I said proudly, as I jiggled Audrey gently in my arms.

Even through my own admittedly biassed eyes, she was beautiful. There was no way they could reject her. And I could see Mrs Stewart was already melting. I remembered how gentle and tender she had been with all the babies she'd fostered when I was younger. She was much more suited to babies, I realised, than to older children.

"Would you like a cuddle?" I asked her, and she nodded eagerly.

"She's a little beauty," she told me.

Mr Stewart, however, stood back and said nothing. It seemed he was immune to the magic of babies, after all.

"Will you bring her again soon?" Mrs Stewart asked, as I was getting ready to leave.

"Of course," I replied.

As I pushed the pram back home, I really wasn't sure whether I was making the right decision, or not. The memory of my mother attacking me in the bathroom was clearer now than it had ever been. Every time I bathed Audrey, I had flashbacks to the assault, her steering me firmly up the stairs, closing the frosted glass door, switching on the taps. In my mind's eye, I could see the row of coloured perfume bottles. Again and again, I swept the images away, like cobwebs. But the reminder was like a wasp, batting against a closed window, looking in vain for a way out. I struggled to shut it out completely.

After all, the attack was the reason I had been taken from my mother and the reason I had grown up in the care system. And yet, in time, I learned to compartmentalise the memory, and push it right to the edge of my mind, so that I could safely look after my daughter. But it was always there, like a hard, cold bullet, lodged in the back of my brain. And for that reason, though it saddened me unspeakably, I had no intention of taking Audrey to see my mother, now or in the future.

I was protective of my daughter, over-protective possibly, and of course I had good cause. Yet still, I did not confront or examine the abuse I had suffered at the Stewart house. In truth, I wasn't even sure that it was abuse; I hadn't allowed myself to think of it in such a way. My mind stalled on the details, like a sputtering car engine, cutting out each time I got close to the facts. And even if it was abuse, then I did not want to think of it, not now. I was safe and cocooned in the perfect bubble of motherhood, and I didn't want to risk puncturing that happiness in any way.

I told myself Mr Stewart had been a strict disciplinarian. I told myself his son had behaved oddly and perhaps a little cruelly. But I went no further. I was good at carrying and hiding secrets. I was really good.

Problem was, I'd gotten too good.

25

Beth Helen

At the end of 1992, when Audrey was four years old, I fell pregnant for a second time. Simon and I were over the moon, and his family, as usual, were delighted and full of offers of help and support. Helen came with me to all my appointments and scans and, when my due date drew nearer, she stepped in to look after Audrey.

"I don't know what I'd do without you," I told her.

Sadly, it wasn't going so well with Simon. After the bliss of having a baby, and then getting married, our relationship had slowly soured, and I began to feel increasingly isolated.

"I just want a normal family," I told him. "You, me and our children."

Perhaps I was expecting too much. We were only young, after all. We were both only 24 years old when I announced my second pregnancy, and by then we had a home, a daughter, and the responsibility of bills and rent. It was too much for us, as a couple. And as my bump grew, the cracks between us grew wider. We bickered and argued a lot. By the time I was five months pregnant, I was seriously starting to think that we needed a break from each other.

"This isn't fair on Audrey," I said. "I don't like arguing in front of her."

Our daughter Beth Helen, named after her grandmother, was born two weeks after her due date, on August 29, 1993. The birth went well, and she was every bit as beautiful as her big sister, though looked nothing like her. Beth was dark, with a round face, and the sweetest dimples. Right from the start, she was such a good baby, and back at home, clucking around my two little chicks, I felt blessed. I had two gorgeous girls to call my own. Never, in those miserable years at the Stewart house, had I ever dreamed I might be so lucky.

"You're Mummy's little stars," I told them.

But Simon and I drifted further apart and when Beth was four weeks old, I made the decision to leave. My own childhood had taught me that my daughters needed to grow up in a happy environment. And the sad reality was that though Simon was a good dad and a decent bloke, we were no longer right for each other.

"We need some time apart," I told him. "A chance to think about what we both really want."

Problem was, I had nowhere to go. I did not want to ask Simon's parents, or any of his family members. I knew they would take us in. But I also understood that I would be putting them in a difficult position, almost asking them to take sides against their own son. I had not seen my own mother since before Audrey was born. And I knew better than to ask Mr and Mrs Stewart.

As I packed my bags, the phone rang. It was Steven. By now he had a partner, Claire, and a place of his own. We had a civil relationship; friendly even. Yes, he had sexually abused me and hurt me. But he had also groomed me and brainwashed me into believing he loved me as a sister. He had shown me what I believed was kindness and support during the worst years of my life, and my subconscious chose to remember that.

"How are you?" he asked. "Me and Claire wondered if we could come and see baby Beth? We could take Audrey out to the park if you like, give you a rest?"

Despite myself, I felt my voice wavering.

"Not great timing, sorry," I mumbled. "Simon and I are having some problems."

Steven listened sympathetically and said:

"Look, we have a spare bedroom. You are welcome to come and stay here until you get yourself sorted."

As I look back now, I want to scream at myself. I want to shout and say:

"Have some dignity, Monica! Show some sense! He abused you! You cannot take your children into his home after what he did to you."

But the abuse was entombed so deeply in my soul that it did not even figure in my thoughts. Conjuring up those memories would have been like calling a spirit back from the grave. It could not be done, not at that time. And after all, what other offers of help did I have? Who else could I turn to? I was alone in the world, now as always. So, I took in a deep breath and said:

"Honestly, that would be so kind, thank you."

I stayed with Steven and Claire for a month, and in that

time, I submitted an application for my own council house. During our stay, Steven was just like a brother towards me. Perhaps he had buried the abuse, as I had. Certainly, I imagine he probably wanted to bury it, for his own sake, if not for mine. Though I had taken steps to find my own house, I still hoped against hope that Simon and I might reconcile, eventually, but it wasn't to be.

"We'll stay friends," we promised each other.

I was offered a neat two-bedroom house, again in East Kilbride, so we were near to Simon and his parents. Though Helen was upset at the break-up, she still helped me settle into the new place and she was as hands-on as ever before. Audrey had started school, so it gave me precious time alone with Beth. The way baby Beth cooed and beamed when she heard Audrey arriving home each afternoon gave me such a warm, complete feeling. It made me so happy that they had each other. I had grown up in a very lonely place and I didn't ever want them to feel isolated or cast out. Slowly, we settled into a new routine. Helen or Simon looked after the girls whilst I worked, first as a hospital domestic and a cleaner, and then, I trained as a phlebotomist. It was a chaotic juggle, as it is for all working mums, but somehow, I managed. Despite the breakdown of our relationship, Simon and I got on well and I knew he wanted to be a good father.

"I know you're doing your best," I told him.

* * * *

One night, when the girls were sleeping over with their grandparents, I called my mother.

"I've just been paid," I said. "Do you fancy going out for tea? My treat?"

Though I didn't want her to see my daughters, I didn't want to abandon her completely. Maybe, on one level, I wanted her to feel proud of me and be pleased that I was doing so well. And, in spite of everything, I wanted to look after her. Behind her malice and spite, she was ill, and she was vulnerable, and undeniably, she needed help. Even though she had tried to kill me, I still wanted to take her out to dinner. It made no sense to me, never mind to anyone else, but I didn't dwell on the logic.

It started off well enough, as social occasions always did with Mum. She had made an effort with her hair and make-up, and, despite years of alcohol abuse, she looked good for her years. She still had a sore knee, and so she limped a little as we climbed the steep stone steps to the Chinese restaurant in Hamilton.

The place was nice inside, nothing fancy, but I felt a swell of pride as we took our seats and examined the menus. I had my wages in a small brown envelope inside my handbag and I wanted to show her that, despite everything, I had made a good life for myself and my children.

"I'll have a vodka and coke," said Mum, snapping her menu shut as the waiter came for our order. "No ice."

Inwardly, I groaned. She never had ice when she was on a bender because she didn't like to dilute the vodka too much. She clearly meant business.

"What else are you having?" I asked her.

"Nothing," she said. "I'll stick to vodka. No food."

I knew better than to argue. My meal came and I ate quietly, whilst she drained one drink after another. The tension grew between us until I felt like I could reach out and touch it. "Don't know why you're wasting good money on food," she grumbled. "We could have eaten at home and spent the cash on a bottle of vodka."

She was getting louder and louder with each complaint, and I felt myself hunching over my plate, folding in, just as I had that first day at school. She had a way of reducing me right down to my most vulnerable state. By the time we were ready to leave, I was cringing with embarrassment. The bill came, and, before I could pay, she snatched it up from the table.

"My God!" she shrieked, knocking her glass flying as she flung out an arm. "Look at the price of this!"

"Mum, please," I mumbled, hastily counting out the notes.

"Hey!" she yelled, right across the restaurant. "No way we're paying this! What a con! You'd better listen to me! Hey! We are not paying!"

I wanted the ground to open and swallow me up, there and then. Fumbling, I left the money on the table and ushered her out, still screeching. I felt so embarrassed. She had ruined a lovely night, and what hurt most was, she hadn't even made an effort. She had set off, right from the start, determined not to eat, determined to spoil it for us both – and for everyone else in the restaurant too. I dreaded to think what all the other customers and staff must have thought.

On the walk back, I dragged behind her, my eyes stinging with tears.

On the surface, we were a mother and daughter, out for a meal and a catch-up. But the reality was very different. I was reminded again of those two telephones, sitting on the sideboard, disconnected from the world.

"What's wrong with you?" my mother slurred.

"Nothing," I said hurriedly. "Nothing at all."

* * * *

I swore that the disastrous encounter with my mother would be my last. I had given her chance after chance, I had forgiven her time after time. All I wanted was some sign, some small indication, that she loved me. But now, as a mother myself, I had to accept that she was most probably incapable of loving anyone – herself included.

In July 1994, I got a call from one of my aunts.

"I'm sorry, Monica, your Mum has passed away," she said. "I appreciate it's a difficult situation, but I thought you should know."

She explained that Mum's body had remained undiscovered in our old home at Hillside Crescent for a number of weeks. It was thought she'd died from an accidental overdose of prescription pills and alcohol. She was only 51 years old.

"Thanks for letting me know," I said quietly.

I felt numb when I put the phone down. It didn't feel right to mourn her, or indeed to not mourn her. She was my mother, the woman who had brought me into the world and given me life. Yet she had neglected me and tried to kill me and condemned me to a miserable childhood in foster care. My love for her was laced through with bitterness and resentment and my feelings were very conflicted and confused. I attended the funeral, a couple of weeks later, but it felt strange and uncomfortable. It was good to see my aunts and Uncle Jerry and yet I felt like an outsider, as though I no longer belonged in this family. Again, I was gripped by that horrible feeling of isolation, so debilitatingly familiar in my younger years. It was a relief to get home to my girls and hold them close. Beth wrapped her chubby arms around my neck, and I hid my face in her hair.

"Missed you, darling," I said.

Mum's death inevitably brought back feelings of sorrow for the mother I might have had. But now I had my own family, it was so much easier to look to the future. Consigning my relationship with Simon to the past too proved much more difficult though. I knew our marriage had run its course.

Yet I felt an almost magnetic pull towards him. Despite our differences, I still loved him, I loved his family, and we had shared so many happy times. More than that, he was the father of my daughters, and I wanted a daddy for them; I craved the traditional family unit that I'd missed out on. I had to consider Simon's parents too, who I looked on as though they were my own. I didn't want to destroy that bond.

I saw Simon quite often, weekly at least, either because of Audrey and Beth or perhaps he would call in to help with tasks around the house.

Funnily enough, we seemed to get on better now that we were living apart. And sometimes, that friendliness spilled over, and we got intimate again.

In March 1996, I discovered I was pregnant.

26

Craig

"Simon, what are we going to do?" I asked him.

Part of me desperately wanted us to give our family life another try. But a bigger part of me knew that would never happen. Our son, Craig Thomas, named after his doting grandfather, was born in December 1996. It was a very difficult delivery, my worst yet, and the labour lasted two days, but felt so much longer. Craig's heartbeat dropped in the final stages and there was panic all around me in the delivery suite. I lost a lot of blood and had to be rushed to theatre, straight after the birth, when the placenta split. It was hugely traumatic, and afterwards, as I cuddled baby Craig in my arms, he screamed solidly. I couldn't seem to comfort him at all.

"He'll calm down, he's just had a shock," smiled my midwife, peering over at Craig's angry little face. "And he looks just like you, Monica. Your double."

I managed to smile back at her, but I felt so weak and washed out. The prospect of coping with three children on my own at home, especially after having surgery, was daunting. But I reminded myself I'd overcome much bigger challenges in the past. As I packed our bags the next morning, ready for home, I felt a little more positive.

"We'll be fine," I told baby Craig, who was still screaming at the top of his lungs. "You'll see."

At home, he cried for five days without stopping and by the end of it, I was frazzled and desperate for sleep. Audrey, eight, and Beth, three, had their hands over their ears every time they walked past his crib.

"What's wrong with the baby, Mummy?" they asked.

"He had a very bumpy ride when he was born," I explained. "He'll quieten down soon, don't worry."

And sure enough, on the sixth day, Craig stopped screaming as suddenly as he'd started, and the relief was glorious. From that moment on, he seemed to be a very contented baby. The girls loved him and fussed over him, and I settled down to life as a single mum of three.

"See?" I smiled at Craig, as I popped him in the pram, ready for the school run. "I told you we'd be just fine! We're better than fine!"

Day by day, it was fascinating to watch the children's personalities emerging. Audrey and Beth were chalk and cheese. Audrey was very talkative and friendly, and still looked just like her daddy. Beth, though quieter, was more self-assured. She was the spokesperson of the family, keen to stand up for us all, and she looked just like Matilda from the children's film. I marvelled at how capable and confident both Audrey and Beth were. They were worlds away from the mixed-up little girl I had once been, which was exactly what I had hoped for.

It was important to me, as the girls grew up, that they saw me earning my own living. I had various jobs, in hospitals and care homes and I was never out of work. And though it was tricky juggling my shifts with the school run and the nursery hours, it was vital to me, as their role model, to always have a job. I wanted my children to have a strong work ethic and to understand that they had to pay their way in the world.

"You can be whatever you want to be," I told them. "But don't rely on anyone except yourself."

I was equally keen for them to do well at school and to not be hamstrung with the same lack of self-belief which had cursed my own childhood. Even as toddlers, I was encouraging them to take an interest in the world around them. I had flashcard words all over the house: 'FRIDGE' on the fridge, 'WASHING MACHINE' on the washer, and so on. There was a note on every item of furniture!

"Mummy, why have we got TELLY on the telly?" Beth asked. "I can't see the screen!"

"Well done!" I clapped. "It does say telly!"

My plan was working perfectly. I was immensely proud that the girls were able to read and write by the time they started school, not because I wanted them to show off or to be top of the class, but simply because I didn't want them to feel in any way lesser or inferior. I knew all too well how that felt, and it hurt.

In the evenings, I was the parent who welcomed all the kids from the street into my home. I'd cook for them all or, in hot weather, I'd take snacks and trays of drinks outside to where they were playing. Often, my thoughts snagged on that single ice-cube Mrs Stewart had given me on that sunny day, long ago, and I smiled bitterly at the memory. I shuddered too, as I remembered Mr Stewart's chilling warning:

'What goes on in this house, stays in this house.'

Well now I was striving for the absolute opposite. I wanted an open house, with no secrets, where everyone was welcome. My kids had sleepovers and friends for tea whenever it was practical. Admittedly, I wasn't so happy for them to sleep over at other houses; I had an acquired and understandable mistrust of strangers, and so I preferred to have my children at home, with me, where I knew they were safe.

I made sure there were lots of activities in our house too. I had pencils and crayons and paints out on the dining table, almost all the time, and we did lots of arts and crafts. The children had Greek cousins on Simon's side of the family and when they flew over to visit, the kids all played together and they slept in one big bed, innocent and happy, as children should be.

Beth joined a girls' football team and each Saturday morning she melted my heart in her red and white striped kit and her long socks which came right over her cute little knees. Win or lose, she always loved to play and afterwards she would trail mud and grass right through my porch and hallway as she gave me a running commentary of her best moves in the match.

"Beth!" I laughed, rolling my eyes.

As I filled the mop bucket, I couldn't help remembering how, at her age, I'd been made to strip off in the cold on the Stewarts' porch to avoid trampling mud or snow from my boots into their home. In the smallest and the most incisive of ways, they made sure that I felt out of place. They made certain that I was not welcome. I was so determined to be nothing like them that I just giggled as Beth made her way up to the bathroom, still in her football boots, still leaving small clumps of mud behind her.

In the summer holidays, my pal, Michelle and I took the kids away on holidays to Lanzarote. They had a great time, in and out of the pool and watching the hotel shows in the evenings. Even though I was totally relaxed, I insisted that the kids wore lifejackets and arm bands.

"You can never be too careful around water," I told them.

I made a big fuss for their birthdays, going over the top with presents, parties and birthday cakes.

"I had a clootie dumpling instead of a cake when I was little," I told my children, and they wrinkled their nose in disgust.

"What presents did you get, Mummy, when you were small?" Beth asked.

I hesitated, not wanting to lie, but not willing to upset her either. I had a sudden flashback to the hateful suitcase for my sixteenth birthday, but I smiled and said:

"One year, I got some coloured pencils, and I drew lovely pictures every day."

On Bonfire night, we wrapped up warm and I took the children out to organised events. As the fireworks popped and banged, I tried to force out the recollections of the time I'd broken the Stewarts' door panel at Halloween and been made to miss the Bonfire celebrations as a punishment.

The run up to Christmas was special in our home, as it always should be. The girls made paper decorations at school, and we hung them on the tree with the same reverence and ceremony as if they were cut from diamonds. The countdown, as Christmas approached, was magical. I especially loved that Craig was a December baby. My favourite times with him were the night feeds that many other mothers disliked so much. But for me, being awake with my baby at 3am, with the Christmas lights twinkling in different colours, and the house peaceful and still, was a moment to savour. Sometimes, I'd put Christmas carols on the stereo, on a low volume. I treasured those nights, just me and my baby boy, and the promise of a wonderful Christmas ahead. I gazed at his perfect little face, marvelled at his tiny hands and feet, and never once took my happiness for granted.

On Christmas Eve, it became a family tradition for us to go to a pantomime and buy an obligatory light-up toy. We always went into town for a festive meal and to admire the Christmas lights. Again, all thoughts of my own miserly Christmas stockings were nudged aside as I wrapped gift after gift for my children. I spoiled them at Christmas, and I was ready to admit it. I made no apology for it.

But deep in the background, in the dimmest rooms of my mind, was an enduring regret that my own childhood had been so barren and so profoundly sad. I didn't dwell in particular on the absence of gifts or treats or celebrations. What I grieved, above all, was the lack of love; the unconditional love, from a mother to a child. I felt that very keenly at Christmas, a time of family love and bonding.

Over the years, since my children were born, I had learned to suppress my fears of bath time and, throughout primary school, we developed an evening routine of bath, supper and bed. I put lavender oil in the children's baths, to soothe and relax them, ready for sleep. When Craig learned to talk, he would shout: "Don't put the oil in, Mummy!" – because he wanted to stay awake all night. It became a running joke in our family.

When he graduated out of night-time nappies, he called his undies his 'big boy pants' and I'd warm a pair on the radiator for him each morning and evening.

"All cosy in my hot pants Mummy!" he'd say, and it always made me laugh.

There was a warm, familial glow in our home. Yet whilst the children splashed and giggled in the bath in the evenings, I battled to banish those images which swam defiantly across my eyeline, the frosted glass, the perfume bottles, the gushing water. I did my best to focus instead on my children's faces and the love that shone from their eyes.

"Come on now, who wants a hot chocolate and a bedtime story?" I asked, holding out a warm towel.

But I could never, no matter how I tried, bring myself to take a bath and instead, I used lavender in the shower. And neither could I bring myself to ever take the children swimming. I had such severe flashbacks, when I walked into the changing rooms of the local leisure centre, that I was practically paralysed with fear. The huge expanse of water – and the associated jeopardy and danger – was too much. Just the smell of the chlorine and the sound of the water splashing was enough to send me dizzy and bring back those horrendous memories of my swimming lessons.

You will learn to swim if it is the last thing I do. I will teach you myself.

I could not bear to be near a swimming pool. I never learned to swim myself and I hated being in water above my knees. Even on holiday, when the kids swam, I had to watch from a distance. It was one scar which, I had to accept, might never heal.

****

By the time Craig turned three years of age, I was starting to worry about his development. He was very fidgety and restless. Unlike his sisters, he couldn't sit still to enjoy a bedtime story or to paint a picture. Though he loved Spiderman, he wasn't able to settle down to watch a film. I hoped he'd grow out of it and that he just needed to improve his concentration. I told myself that maybe it was a boy thing, that he preferred tearing around the house to sitting quietly with a colouring book or doing a jigsaw. But in truth, I felt pretty sure that it was more serious than that.

Around this time, we moved to a bigger house, with three bedrooms. It was in the same area but there was more space and a little garden for the children. I was offered a new job as a private carer in a large and opulent house nearby. The money was good, it was a significant pay-rise, and it was just what I needed, especially with the expense of our new home. But the work was night shifts only and that was a big drawback for me with my childcare problems.

"I have three young children," I explained to my employer.

It was agreed that the two girls could sleep there overnight, in the same room as me and I could take them straight to school after my shift finished each morning. Craig, however, was a trickier proposition. He never went to bed without a fuss each night, he was noisy and boisterous, and it often took me an hour or two to settle him. There was no way I could take him to work with me, less still have him sleep there overnight; I'd lose my job within the week. I didn't know what to do.

There was nobody I could ask to help out. Simon was busy with his own job. I saw less of his family these days too. My thoughts, somehow, drifted to Mrs Stewart; to how gentle and kind she'd been with the babies and toddlers she'd fostered in the past, and I wondered if she might perhaps look after him for me. She had only met Craig once, as a baby. But I was desperate, I needed this job to pay my bills. Her own children had long since moved out of the family home and it was just her and Mr Stewart left now. Swallowing my pride, and plucking up courage, I dialled their number.

"I'd love to look after Craig," she said immediately. "I remember him well."

And so, on my way to my night shift, three times a week, I began dropping Craig off with Mrs Stewart. Before long, he was calling her 'Gran' and he saw the whole experience as a fun sleepover. She seemed to have endless patience with him. When I explained to her that I was worried about his concentration and his behaviour, she waved away my worries with a maternal smile. "I can manage Craig," she promised me. "Don't you worry."

The arrangement lasted for a few months. I know that Craig was happy with Mrs Stewart and there were no flash-points, in fact no problems at all. But looking back, I cannot understand what possessed me to let that woman baby-sit my son and I will never forgive myself for leaving him in their care. My only defence is that, back then, I had not yet acknowledged or confronted the trauma I'd suffered under that roof. I did not recognise that it was abuse. It was so deeply interred in my memory that I never once considered that the family was not one I could or should trust. I was coping, the best way I could, juggling the demons of the past and the demands of the present. I appreciate this is hard for others to understand. It is harder still for me. That guilt, that shame, of letting my own children down is worse than anything I went through myself as a child, and I will always regret my decision to allow them to look after my son. I accept that people might judge me, but nobody will judge me more harshly than I do myself.

I have often tortured myself, wondering whether me allowing Mr Stewart to babysit my son was the ultimate victory for him. He had fooled most people with his façade of religious piety. Had he fooled me also?

I was not sorry when, before Craig turned four, I was able to find a day job which fitted in around school and nursery hours. It was a more suitable arrangement all round. Craig started school in September 2001, and it was worrying, but no surprise, when his teachers called me in for a meeting.

"He just can't sit still," they said. "He can't concentrate. He seems to struggle to process simple instructions."

"I know," I replied. "I've been concerned about this for a couple of years."

They referred Craig for help and arranged for a psychologist to sit in the classroom to observe him. A year on, he was finally diagnosed with ADHD. Naively, I hoped that the diagnosis would be a step forwards, a chance for us to access appropriate help. But instead, as time passed, it felt more like a label, marking him out without really offering any support.

"Why am I not the same as my friends?" he asked me sadly. "I don't want to be different."

I could only hug him in reply. It was frustrating, because on a one-to-one basis, Craig was a quick learner. At home, for very short spells, I made real progress with him. But he could not concentrate for long and he could not cope in big groups. And so in a classroom, with other children, he was way out of his depth. I worried so much about the future, about how he'd manage at high school, and beyond. Outside of education, he was a loving and affectionate little boy, with boundless energy and a brilliant sense of humour. He made everybody around him laugh and he had lots of friends. He was a born entertainer.

But I had to keep an eye on him all of the time. He was forever getting into scrapes or running off whilst we were out. He had no understanding of rules or of danger and it was exhausting, just making sure that I kept him safe.

One of my tactics was to try to keep him busy, thinking I might be able to tire him out and steer him away from mischief. I enrolled him in all sorts of classes, football teams, ice-skating, drama club. But though he loved them all at first, none of them lasted because Craig couldn't concentrate or follow instructions. In particular, he showed a talent for drama. But eventually, he was asked to leave the class.

"It's such a shame that his attention span is so short," the teacher said. "He's really good at drama. We'll miss him so much."

I tried another club, and another. But it was hard to get Craig to stick at anything for long. Keeping him occupied and out of trouble was a full-time occupation in itself, and it was draining, especially alongside my other responsibilities.

27

Melanie

When Craig was five, I met a new partner, John, and we fell in love. John moved us all out to a beautiful house in the Ayrshire countryside, where the children had huge bedrooms and even a living room all of their own. John generously took us away on several holidays in a year, to different areas of Spain. And although, or perhaps because, it was a complete change of routine, Craig loved those trips. He seemed like a totally different child and his behaviour was impeccable whilst we were abroad. Freed from the rules and regulations of school, and away from the pressure to conform, he was, for once, a typically carefree little boy. He loved running on the beach, making sandcastles, and paddling in the sea. He was happiest when he was free. But as soon as we returned home, his problems surfaced once again.

"He can't cope with being hemmed in, with the routine of education," I worried. "But I don't know how to help him."

When Craig was seven, John and I decided to separate, and the kids and I found ourselves in temporary accommodation for a couple of weeks, before I found a new two-bedroom flat. It was a big adjustment after the beautiful house and all the luxuries we'd left behind. But my experiences had taught me that money and material possessions were not important. The holidays and the big house were lovely, sure. But my children had to come first. At the earliest suggestion of trouble in a relationship, no matter what the financial fall-out, I knew I had to walk away.

The following year, I met a new partner, Chris, and mid-way through 2004, aged 36, I fell pregnant. It was unplanned, but I was pleased. A new life was always a reason to celebrate. I expected my pregnancy to go without a hitch, just like the other three. And for the first few months, everything was normal and going to plan. A scan showed that I was carrying a little girl, and Audrey, Beth and Craig were all thrilled, excitedly squabbling over names and over who would have the first cuddle.

"You can all have the first cuddle," I smiled.

But at around 10pm on January 6, 2005, when I was seven months pregnant, my waters broke. I had sat down briefly on the end of the bed, to pull my trousers off, and that was when I felt it; a familiar and frightening gush of fluid.

"Chris!" I yelled, in sheer panic.

Chris dashed into the bedroom, took one look at the puddle on the carpet, and called his mother to look after the children. We rushed to Wishaw General Hospital, and I held my breath anxiously, whilst I was scanned and examined.

"You're four centimetres dilated and already in the early stages of labour," said a doctor. "We'll do what we can to slow the contractions down."

I was hooked up to a drip, and also given steroids to

strengthen the baby's lungs. But as the hours passed, my labour pains grew stronger. We were told there was no choice but to deliver our baby. She was on her way, she was coming, and all we could do was hope. Then came more bad news.

"We've no incubators free here," the doctor said. "You will need to give birth elsewhere."

I was transferred to Ninewells Hospital, in Tayside, an agonising 40-minute journey in the ambulance which seemed, to me, to last forever. Early the following morning, after a consultation with a new doctor, we were told our baby had just a fifty percent chance of survival.

"We have to focus on the positive," I said to myself. "She can make it. She can."

My labour was stop-start all day, but the pain was nothing compared to the worry and distress I felt inside.

"She can make it," I said again to myself.

I felt that if I stayed upbeat, she'd somehow hear me, and take strength from me. But deep down, I think I already knew what lay ahead. Late that night, the contractions intensified. Our daughter, Melanie, was born at 12.55am and, as she was delivered, a midwife whisked her away quickly into another room. I saw a glimpse of bluish skin, a tiny turned up nose, and then she was gone. She did not cry. She did not make a sound. That silence, more than anything, would haunt me forever.

"How is she?" I asked. "Can I see her?"

But nobody could say. The wait was torture. Around twenty minutes later, a doctor came into the delivery suite, carrying the tiniest bundle, wrapped in a soft blanket.

"I am so sorry," he said. "I really am. We did all we could. The cord was around her neck, and she is very tiny. She couldn't be saved."

The pain in my chest expanded so quickly, it felt like a heart-attack. Chris and I clung to each other, as though we might collapse and disintegrate if we were pulled apart.

"I really am sorry," the doctor said again, as he held Melanie out towards me, his arms outstretched.

"No," I wept. "I can't see her. I can't hold her."

I was terrified of looking at her face. Petrified of what I might see and never unsee.

"I think you may regret it if you don't hold her, skin to skin," the doctor urged. "This is your chance to say goodbye. Please think about it, Monica."

Eventually, still sobbing, I extended my arms. I was shaking with nerves, and yet, the moment I held her, they simply dissolved, and I was overcome with love. She was warm and soft, not at all how I had expected. And she was beautiful too. Flawless in every way. She had fair hair and was quite tall; her legs were so long that they draped past my stomach and down my side. Gently, I unwrapped the blanket and held her fingers and toes. I admired her hands and feet. I kissed the tip of her tiny nose. She was a tiny vision of absolute perfection.

"Wake up, Melanie," I pleaded. "Please wake up, darling."

I begged her over and over again. The tears streamed down my cheeks and onto her cheeks, and I wiped them gently dry with my thumb.

"Please wake up," I whispered again.

By now, I was sobbing uncontrollably great, heaving cries that racked my entire body. My baby would never wake up. Never. It felt so cruel, so incredibly unfair.

"You will always be my angel," I vowed. "I will always love you, every minute of every hour. We will be together again, I promise, one day."

Alongside the intolerable grief, as the minutes passed, was a growing sense of anger and injustice. Hadn't I been through enough in my life, without losing my baby? I'd come to terms with what I'd suffered as a child myself, because the gift of motherhood had helped to ease my pain and to heal my scars. I needed my children, just as much as they needed me. Yet now, my own child had been stolen from me.

"Where is the humanity?" I raged. "Who would take a baby girl away from her mother, before her first breath?"

I thought of all those Sundays, with the Stewarts, worshipping God. I remembered the night-time prayers, the devout faith, the ruinous guilt. It had all been for nothing. God, in that moment, was without compassion and without love. In vain, I reached out, through my pain, for memories of my beloved Granny, for some solace and hope.

Never forget you are loved, Monica.

But I did not feel loved. I felt forgotten and abandoned. I felt godless and lost. I felt as though I was cursed.

Later that day, we were taken to a lovely, light room with two big leather chairs, a sofa bed, and even an ensuite bathroom. At the side of the room was an incubator. Melanie was already inside, waiting for us, washed and dressed and wearing the cutest knitted pink cardigan and matching hat.

She looked adorable; and absolutely perfect too. It was just as though she was sleeping. I was told the clothes were made specially for babies who were born sleeping and I felt a rush of gratitude towards the kind soul who had donated them.

Chris and I spent the rest of the day and the following night with Melanie in that room. At times, cruelly, unbearably, I thought I heard her whimper, and I rushed to the cot to check on her. Gazing at her beautiful face I could almost convince myself that she was simply having a nap, that she was healthy and well, and that we would soon be taking her home to her doting siblings. But as the hours passed, and the new day dawned, her cheeks began to bruise, and her skin became discoloured. It felt as though she was dying – slipping away – right in front of my eyes. I had been praying, begging, hoping for a miracle; a resurrection. But it was not to be.

"I'm sorry, darling," I wept.

The following morning, we were allowed to return to Wishaw Hospital, with Melanie, on our own. I found it surprising and more than a little daunting, but the nurses explained it was another step in our grieving process. Chris carried her tiny Moses basket out to the car whilst I said goodbye and thank you to the maternity staff, whose kindness and support I would cherish always. I sat in the back seat, with Melanie, on the journey. In some ways, I wanted it over with; I was consumed with pain, trapped in a bottomless pool of sorrow. But another part of me wanted that journey to last forever; just me and my baby, together in the back of the car, until the end of time. I didn't want to face the end.

"Are you OK?" Chris kept asking, nodding at me through the driver's mirror.

He was torn in two himself, I knew, and yet he was doing his best to support me. We arrived at the hospital and, as we pulled into the main car park, it suddenly hit me, like a sledgehammer.

How on earth could we carry Melanie from the car, through the hospital, and up the stairs to the maternity unit, where the staff were waiting for us? We were staring at a logistical and emotional time-bomb.

"What if someone looks in the Moses basket?" I asked Chris. "What should we say?"

He looked as scared and as lost as I was. We sat motionless in the car for almost an hour, the silence sagging and stretching between us, before he said:

"Right, on the count of three, we'll get out of the car. I will carry Melanie, let's just keep our heads down. Nobody will bother us. One, two, three…"

I was so grateful for his strength and, as we walked across the tarmac, carrying our precious cargo, I folded into him, leaning my head on his shoulder. It was as though my legs could no longer hold me up unaided. We arrived at the entrance foyer and, as I made my way through the double doors, I heard a voice shout:

"Monica! Hey – you've had the baby then! Let's see!"

I rotated slowly, almost mechanically, to come face to face with the brother of one of my good pals. Of course, he wasn't to know about our loss.

"Congratulations!" he smiled. "What did you have?"

Chris hurried off ahead, carrying Melanie in the Moses basket, and I stuttered:

"Yes, thank you, we had a baby girl. Sorry, I'm in a rush."

I dashed off and through a blur of tears, I thought of the disconnected telephones of my childhood. I thought of my dead baby, in her Moses basket. Nothing was as it seemed. Why was my life like this? Why was I damned to suffer? Somehow, we made it upstairs to the ward where we were taken to a small room.

"It's time to say goodbye and leave Melanie here," said a midwife.

The idea of leaving her behind was unbearable; insurmountable. I didn't think I could say goodbye. I just couldn't do it. What mother can ever say goodbye to her child? On either side of her Moses basket, Chris and I held Melanie's hands and kissed her little cheeks. I thought of her first smile, her first steps, her first day at school. Of her prom, of her first boyfriend, of her wedding day. All cruelly ripped away from her, and from me.

"I am sorry, darling," I sobbed. "I love you. Mummy loves you."

She was by now stone cold, and her face was discoloured. She no longer looked at all like herself.

"Time to go," Chris whispered, hugging me tightly. "The kids are waiting for us at my mum's. It's time to go."

Walking out of that room was the hardest thing I had ever done. Inside, I was screaming at myself.

"Don't walk away! She's your baby! You're her Mummy!"

Only Chris's hands, gently steering me forwards, prevented

me from running back and throwing myself down next to her. And when we got home, the pain only sharpened. Beth and Craig crowded round me with inevitable questions.

"Where's the baby? Where's Melanie?"

Craig, eight, had been really looking forward to our new arrival. He kissed my tummy every night before bed. He had been so excited about his new sister. Beth, eleven, was naturally bright and inquisitive and full of questions I could not answer.

"But where exactly is she?" she asked. "What happened to her? Can we say goodbye? Who is with her now?"

The questions were tough, but she had to work through her grief, just as I did, and I tried to be patient.

"She's with the angels," I told her softly. "And she will always be in our hearts too."

Days later, Melanie was buried at Priestfield Cemetery in Hamilton, with a short service attended only by me and Chris. I felt it would be too upsetting for the children to come. Losing Melanie was heart-breaking for them, and confusing too. And for Chris and I, it was a real test. We had been together only a few months when I fell pregnant, our relationship was still, in many ways, a fledgling one, and yet we had been through so much together. We tried to be strong for each other, but we mourned in different ways, and I knew our grief was pulling us apart.

28

Georgia

In April, just three months after Melanie died, I missed a period. When a test showed I was pregnant, I put my face in my hands and cried.

"I'm too frightened to have another baby," I said to Chris. "What if it happens again? I can't go through with it."

And yet, I knew I had to. I reminded myself that each new life was precious and that I needed to look forwards. We were very cautious and careful as my bump grew, especially as I approached seven months, the point where I had lost Melanie. The children were excited again, and I tried to manage their giddiness, just in case. Just in case. Each night, my dreams were filled with images and reminders of Melanie. Sometimes, I'd wake from a nightmare, feeling sure I was going to lose this baby too. I had extra checks and scans at the hospital, and, at seven months, a routine check showed that I was 4cm dilated, just as I had been at seven months with Melanie.

"No!" I gasped. "Not again!"

"You need to rest, completely," the doctors told me. "We'd like to admit you into hospital, total bed rest, until the baby is born."

I shook my head. There was no way I could leave Craig and Beth, they needed me too. I agreed I would rest at home and would return immediately to the maternity unit if my labour began. Incredibly, in the peace of my own home, the bed rest seemed to work, and, as the days rolled slowly into weeks and months, I allowed myself to get a tiny bit excited. By the time my due date came, I couldn't wait to meet our new baby.

Our daughter, Georgia, was born naturally, on December 5, 2005. She was gorgeous and angelic, and I knew she was a gift from her big sister in the sky. This was Melanie's way of keeping in touch with us all; this was her early Christmas gift to us all.

"Thank you, darling," I murmured.

I loved having another December baby too; those days before Christmas were very special, as I juggled wrapping gifts and attending nativity plays with night-time feeds under the glow of the Christmas lights. Uncle Jerry heard that I'd had a new baby and he came to visit, with his wife and two children. It was lovely to see him; always. One look at his warm smile and I was back on the window ledge, swinging my legs, breathing in the smell of petrol. He was a good man and had shown me real kindness when I was little. Yet despite that, as we chatted, I still felt very much like the odd one out; like that side of my life had moved on without me, and I could no longer catch up or fit in. My mother's sister visited too and brought a gift for Georgia. And later, she invited me to a family gathering.

"I'd love to come," I said. "I'd like to see everyone again."

But in reality, I was dreading it. Much as I wanted to step back and be little Monica again, pinching my aunt's fur coat for the rag and bone man, or feeding coins into the electric meter, I just couldn't do it. There was a brick wall between me and my early life. It was one I had built myself, in order to survive and I could not now smash it down on a whim. Everyone at the party was welcoming and friendly and there were lots of hugs and kisses. But I only stayed a short time. I didn't belong here. Not anymore.

"Too much time has passed," I said sadly to myself.

When Georgia was two, Chris and I split up. Since losing Melanie, we'd struggled to reconnect. We'd both mourned her separately and there was a gaping void between us. By this time, Audrey had moved out into her own place, so I was on my own again, with Beth, Craig and Georgia.

"We'll manage," I told them. "We always do, somehow."

But Craig's behaviour problems, in and out of school, were becoming intolerable. He found academic work so challenging that he began playing truant from lessons. And yet in other ways he was very intelligent. He was extremely practical and had a gift for making and building things. Once, I had a new living room door delivered and I was waiting for a joiner to come and hang it. But Craig, though he was only ten years old, worked out how to do it all by himself.

"Craig, that's amazing," I smiled. "You're so clever."

Another time, I bought him a kit to make an ornamental ferris wheel. The recommended age range was sixteen plus and there was a warning on the box that it would take two people to build. But Craig, again just ten years old, assembled it on his own without an issue. I was so proud of him and yet it made me sad that his talents were not recognised at school or more broadly in education. He was just known as 'the boy with the problems' and I felt that nobody really looked beyond that. I was reminded, yet again, of the telephones from my childhood. Nothing was as it seemed on the surface.

Rejected and alienated by the system, Craig became frustrated and isolated, and as the months passed, he struggled more and more. He was a funny little boy; he could always make people laugh with his expressions or his jokes. Yet he was very vulnerable and fragile too. When he fell in with a group of older boys, my heart sank. He'd wait for me to go to work each morning and then instead of going to school, he'd hang around with lads who were four or five years older than him.

Next, he started drinking. Some evenings, he didn't come home. I was out of my mind with worry, searching the local parks and the streets in the dark, whilst Beth looked after Georgia for me back at the house. One night, I found him with a bunch of fifteen-year-old boys, and he was blind drunk.

"Do you know how old he is?" I asked them crossly. "You should send him home, not buy him booze."

The problem was, Craig was so easily led astray, and, to the older boys, he was entertaining and comical when he was drunk. They found it hilarious to fill him full of cider and Craig certainly did not object.

"It's dangerous to drink at your age," I told Craig. "I want you to stop. Please."

"I promise," he replied. "I'm sorry Mum. It won't happen again."

It wasn't that Craig was naughty. It was simply that he couldn't make his own decisions. His promises were genuine and sincere, I knew that. But the following day, I found him drunk again. I frog-marched him home and grounded him. Over the months, I tried punishment, bribery, tough love and overindulgence. But nothing worked. Craig's problems were becoming more and more demanding and time-consuming, and I barely had time to look after Beth and Georgia, or to go to work. One evening, a policeman brought him home.

"We found your son lying in the road, under the influence," he said. "Try and keep him under control."

"I am trying," I said wearily. "I really am."

Another time, Craig was found almost unconscious in a field. He was taken to hospital for checks and luckily, after he slept the booze off, he was fine. But I was at my wits' end, frantic with worry that he would hurt himself, or worse.

"Please Craig, you have to stop this," I said.

But he didn't know how. He just couldn't help himself. And of course, at the back of my mind, was the echo of my teenage self, drinking my way to oblivion, night after night. My own mother had been an alcoholic. I'd had a drink problem as a teenager. And now my own son. I felt as though the sins of the mothers were being passed down through the generations, onto my precious boy.

The triggers for our drinking were undeniably different; I was drinking to blot out abuse, rejection, unhappiness. Craig was drinking because he had behavioural disorders. But there were glaring similarities too, between Craig and I, and that hurt me terribly. We both felt alienated and shut out; we both felt that the system had failed us. I didn't want any of my children to follow the same path as me and to suffer as I had. More than anything, I wanted to protect Craig and keep him safe and yet I felt like he was moving further and further away from me.

2010 - 2022
THE SUPREME COURT, LONDON

29

The Social Worker Visit

Aged eleven, after several hospital admissions for drinking, it was decided that Craig should be admitted to a specialist unit at Yorkhill Children's Hospital, Glasgow. His doctors explained that they were hoping to identify a trigger for his behaviours, and to understand the pattern they followed. He stayed in hospital from Monday to Friday each week and, every evening, the girls and I would get two buses, right across the city, to visit him.

By now, I was working day shifts as a senior carer, and it was always a rush to make it in time to collect Beth from school and Georgia from nursery, before running to the bus stop, their hands in mine. Often it was nearly 9pm by the time we got home, and I'd rustle up a quick meal before tucking Georgia into bed or helping Beth with a bit of homework. It was hectic and exhausting. And yet, it wasn't all miserable. The girls really enjoyed those bus journeys, drawing on the misted-up windows with their fingers or waving at cars passing by. On Fridays, we'd have a takeaway treat on our way home, or we'd stop for a Chinese buffet, our family favourite. And I think, too, the girls benefited from the respite; it was stressful for them with Craig at home. We lurched from one drama to another and there was little time or consideration for anyone else. As much as they missed and loved their brother, they also appreciated the peace.

Craig, surprisingly, quite enjoyed staying in the unit. He made friends and he preferred it there, certainly over going to school, where he felt he didn't fit in and the teachers had given up on him. For me, though I missed him terribly, it was a relief that he was away from the influences of the older kids and the alcohol. I hoped this might be a turning point for him. It was a full year before Craig was discharged from hospital, aged twelve. But sadly, and infuriatingly, his doctors could offer me no solutions.

"We can't find the trigger for Craig's behaviours," they said. "We believe he has a personality disorder but he's too young for an official diagnosis."

After Craig came home from the unit, I was so glad of the support of social services. I had always been wary of social workers, given my past experiences, yet I knew Craig needed more help than I could give him. And the social worker who was assigned to us was nothing like the characters I remembered from my childhood; she was kind and supportive and practical too.

"You've a lot on your plate, Monica," she told me. "I'm just here to try and ease the burden if I can."

But Craig's behaviour deteriorated further and further. He fell back in with the older boys, much to my frustration. And, with no outlet for his angst, he began drinking more and getting into scrapes. Friends and neighbours, and even the police, were forever knocking on the door to tell me about his latest transgression.

"Why are you behaving like this?" I asked Craig. "You're putting yourself at risk."

But he shrugged. He had no answers. I felt my heart clenching with anxiety. I was losing him; I could feel it. He was sliding way out of my reach.

"Come here," I said, wrapping my arms around him. "You know I love you and I always will."

By hugging him close, I told myself that I could somehow keep him safe. But I was kidding myself. On one level, he was still my sweet, funny little boy. He was as affectionate and loving as ever. But he had such serious problems that he was putting himself and others at risk, and I felt totally out of my depth. Some evenings, he stayed out way later than he was allowed, on occasions, he didn't come home at all. Night after night, I didn't sleep. I paced the bedroom floor, praying that he was safe but imagining all sorts of horrific scenarios. Every time I heard a distant siren, I felt my insides twisting in panic. Was that for my boy?

"Where have you been?" I shrieked when he finally showed up, drunk but unharmed. "I've been worried out of my mind!"

But he just didn't get it. I was under so much pressure, and, as hard as I tried to keep it all together, I could feel myself crumbling. Bit by bit, chip by chip, I was losing my grip.

One afternoon, early in 2009, Craig's social worker came to the house. Craig wasn't at home, but she wanted to see me.

"How are you coping?" she asked.

"I'm finding it very hard," I admitted. "I feel like I spend all my time looking after Craig and yet I don't feel like I'm helping him. He's getting worse, not better. I'm missing out on the girls. They're missing out on me. I'm falling asleep at work. I'm too exhausted to cook and clean. I don't know what to do for the best."

Even as I spoke, the tears spilled down my cheeks.

"What about a children's unit?" the social worker suggested. "If Craig went into our care, on a temporary basis, it would give you all a chance to regroup, including Craig."

Her words were like a punch right under my ribs.

"Care?" I stuttered. "You want to take my son into care?"

It made sense. I knew that. Craig needed specialist help. My daughters needed my attention. I needed a break. But the idea of my own child going into care – after what I had been through – was a savage blow. In that moment, I was transported back through the years and there I was, aged five, standing on the Stewarts' doorstep with my baby's bottle in my hand.

What goes on in this house, stays in this house.

I saw the big chunks of ham in the toilet bowl. I heard the footsteps, thirteen in all. I felt the clammy anticipation of a beating.

"No!" I yelled suddenly. "No!"

The room swam around me as the tears flowed, like one continuous stream, down my face. And before I knew it, the memories of my past came tumbling out, insistent, violent, as if a volcano had erupted right there in my living room.

"I was badly treated in care myself," I sobbed. "Beaten and battered. I was pushed out. I was unloved and unwanted. I can't have that for my son. I can't."

The social worker listened in open-mouthed horror as I described how, at the Stewarts, we had all been lined up, in height ascending order, for military inspections. How we had lived in fear of the mythical lie detector test. How I was beaten black and blue because my arithmetic was poor or because I failed to eat my Sunday lunch.

"My foster father always told me I'd amount to nothing," I wept. "And look at me. My own son is going into care. He was right, after all. He's won."

I felt so helpless, so wretched. So defeated.

"Craig would only go into the children's home on a temporary basis, to give you some respite," the social worker explained. "It's a completely different situation, Monica. We think it's the best way of keeping him safe.

"You can still see him. He can still come home. This is no reflection on you as a mother or on Craig. None whatsoever."

I wanted to believe her. But in truth, I could hardly take her words in. I felt physically wounded. My mind was swirling with images of Mr and Mrs Stewart, of the Saturday night preparations for church, the Sunday morning rigmarole, the night-time prayers. After years of blocking it out, so efficiently, my head was now bursting with memories, sharp in focus and deeply painful.

"I think you ought to speak to the police and perhaps also Victim Support," the social worker added. "I can help you to make the complaint. You have carried this for too long, Monica."

On one level, the prospect of speaking to a complete stranger about my childhood was so alarming that it felt impossible to do. And yet, now that I had uncorked my memories, I could not simply squeeze them back in. They were buzzing around, inside my head, with more, many more, waiting to emerge. I knew I had to do something. In a way, I had been expecting this and preparing for it. The time had come.

First, I had to confide in my children. Georgia was only three years old and far too young for this. But I gathered my older girls together and told them the truth about my childhood. We wept together; they cried for me and I for them.

"How could you go through this on your own?" Beth asked me. "Why didn't you tell us?"

"I suppose I was trying to protect you," I replied. "And myself also. I wanted to be a good mum and a good role model. I felt like I couldn't confront the abuse because it would have destroyed me and it would have affected me as a mum. I wanted to focus on you, and on the future."

It was quite some time later when I told Craig. I was wary of over-burdening him because he had his own issues to contend with. But I also knew he deserved the truth.

"Why did you go back to see Mr and Mrs Stewart after the way they treated you?" he asked me, bewildered. "I don't understand it. You even let them baby-sit for me!"

I hung my head.

"If there is one thing I could change, from my entire childhood, it would be that," I said softly. "I am so sorry Craig. I love you more than anything and I would never knowingly put you in danger of any kind.

"Back then, I didn't recognise the abuse for what it was. That's all I can say. But I will never forgive myself."

He put his arms around me.

"I forgive you," he said. "And that should be enough. Forget it, Mum. You've been through too much already."

Again, despite everything, despite the torrent of pain I had unleashed in my memory, I felt blessed. I was so lucky to have such wonderful children. They had saved me over and over again and they were still saving me now.

30

Hear My Voice

I was a bundle of nerves when two CID officers knocked on the door some weeks later. My friend, Carol, had offered to be with me and I needed her support, now more than ever.

"Basically, we'd like you to start from the beginning and tell us what happened," they said.

I took in the deepest of breaths. I had carried my memories for so long, mostly dormant but always bubbling, always threatening to burst through the surface.

"I arrived on their doorstep with nothing more than a baby's bottle," I told them sadly. "And even that was taken away from me."

Through choking sobs, I told them all about Mr Stewart, the beatings, the mental cruelty, the total lack of love.

"That's what hurt me most," I wept. "The absence of affection was worse than the physical abuse."

On and on, the memories poured out, like a burst geyser. My account was relayed in such astonishing detail that I felt as though I was back there again, in the Stewart house, with the speckled carpet, the brown curtains, the bunk beds, and my song:

"In a big house in a green field
Far far away!
In a garden with my family
Far far away!"

I described Steven's behaviour towards me, as a small child; the grooming, the brainwashing, the excruciating sexual abuse in my own bed, in my own home, in the one place I should have been safe.

"It was a bad thing. Maybe it was even worse than I thought."

When I had finished speaking, Carol said to me: "Monica, you are describing the sexual assault of a child. That's horrific."

She was crying too. I looked at her not wanting to believe it, and yet simultaneously knowing that it was true. I could not explain it. I was furiously shaking my head yet agreeing with her, all at once.

Again, even though I could not argue against her, I did not quite believe her. I hoped there was a different, more palatable label for what I had suffered, less damning, less damaging. I did not want to condemn my foster brother as a sexual abuser. And neither did I want to be a victim of childhood sexual abuse. The truth was out. But still, I could not face it, not fully.

My interview lasted the entire day and though it was painful and painstaking, it was also immensely cathartic and cleansing. I gave a clear outline of my life, from aged five to seventeen, in as much detail as I could recall. There were some incidents and some situations which were still too deeply buried. There were also some memories which I was too ashamed to share. I understand now, from a rational viewpoint, that I had, and still have, no reason to feel any disgrace or humiliation. Yet the shame hovered over me, spectre-like, refusing to budge.

You'll never amount to anything, Monica.

The police officers were kind and patient and yet I was shaking and trembling throughout the whole ordeal. They promised to investigate and to report back to me as soon as possible.

"There were loads of other children in the foster home," I told them. "You should try and contact them. They could confirm some of the incidents that happened there."

One of the officers urged me to speak to Victim Support, just as the social worker had done.

"They will help you access your social services records," she said. "You may find counselling is helpful. This is a lot for you to go through, Monica, on your own. It's time to accept some help."

* * * *

It would be another few weeks before I made an appointment with Victim Support, and I was assigned a counsellor called Gwen. Together, we filled out the necessary paperwork to apply for access to my social services files. When they arrived, I didn't even dare open the envelope. Instead, I called in to see Gwen.

"Monica, these files are truly shocking," she told me, as she read page after page. "I really think you ought to instruct a lawyer."

I was taken aback.

"Why would I need a lawyer?" I asked, bewildered. "I don't understand."

She handed me the files for me to read myself, and recommended a solicitor, Paul Brown, of the Legal Services Agency, in Glasgow.

"Have a think about it, Monica," she said. "Please don't let this go. You deserve justice."

I still didn't understand what she meant. Late that night, with the kids in bed and some time to myself, I made a cup of tea and opened the files. It was very odd, reading about my childhood. It was as though I was in some way removed and distant from it all. And it was unbearably sad too. I wanted to reach into the pages, to that poor little girl, and say:

"Come with me. I'll look after you. I'll love you."

To my disgust, I came across comments from social workers which suggested they knew that I was unhappy. There were references made to me picking at my skin and seeming upset, though they seemed to presume that my visits home were more upsetting than my time in foster care. In January 1986, a social worker commented:

'Monica is quiescent and non-assertive in her manner. She does not seem safe/secure enough to challenge her foster parents (who are strong characters) unlike the other members of the family.'

Why, if they suspected something was wrong, did they leave me there, month after month, year after year? I had spent my entire childhood believing that nobody had noticed me, that nobody knew. My blood boiled as I realised that maybe my sadness was evident after all. Yet, quite unforgivably, they had ignored it and they ignored me.

"Why?" I asked myself out loud. "Why didn't they ask me what was wrong? Why didn't they take me out of that house?"

I flipped over the page and, there, in stark black and white, were the details of the attack by my mother:

'On August 2 1973, in Lanark Sheriff Court, Mrs Mount was convicted of (attempted murder) in that on July 4 1973 in the bathroom of the house occupied by Andrew Russell, she did assault Monica Mount and did seize and compress her throat with her hands, all to her injury. Mrs Mount pleaded guilty and was sentenced to 18 months to run from July 25 1973.'

This was the first time I'd ever seen the cold facts written down. It was validation, actual, tangible proof, if any were needed, of what my mother had done. I was shivering so hard that I dropped the papers and covered my face with my hands. I closed my eyes, reliving the attack in broken fragments; the perfume bottles, the frosted glass in the door, my mother's ragged fingernails as she switched on the taps. I could feel her bony hands around my throat, even now, squeezing tighter and tighter… Her face loomed before me. I gasped a little.

This was the worst part, I told myself, taking in a deep breath. It was over now. I had read it. Steadying myself, I opened the file again and scanned down the page. Quite suddenly, my blood iced over. The words seemed at once to blur into one and also to jump off the page at me. They were brutally clear and yet horribly bewildering too:

'On July 11 1968 at Lambeth Magistrates Court, Mrs Mount was convicted of Attempted Murder, reduced to Wilful Assault and Causing Unnecessary Suffering (to Monica Mount) and sentenced to three years' probation with the condition of residence at her Mother's House.'

I read it again and again, my heart pounding, wondering if I had somehow made a mistake. Yet it was screamingly obvious. It was too monstrous, too wicked, for words. My mother had attacked me twice – once in the bathroom, and also once before as a baby. I was just five months old, in July 1968, at the time of sentencing. I remembered being told that we had lived for a period with my grandparents when I was a baby. But I'd had no idea it was as part of a court directive. I also knew my mother had lived in London for a short time immediately after I was born, hence the trial at Lambeth magistrates.

Gwen's words came back to me:

"You should get yourself a lawyer."

They were starting to make a sickening sort of sense now. Because why on earth after she had tried to kill me once, was my mother allowed to have me back in her care? She had gone on to attack me again, to try to drown me, and yet even then she was still allowed to see me. The social workers had, on occasion, left me on my own with my mother, during my visits home, despite her having twice tried to kill me. It was outrageous and staggering, the stuff of nightmares. I had no idea of the details of the first attack, and, that night in bed, my mind swarmed with possibilities. I had no obvious physical scars, and no long-term health conditions, which might have arisen from an attempt on my life. To my knowledge I hadn't spent time in hospital as a baby, though this could have been kept from me, as everything else clearly was. Through the early hours, as I lay wide awake, I endured ghastly visions of my mother dangling me out of a window or dropping me into a bath or pushing my pram down a hill and watching it crash. What could it be? How did she try to kill me? Again and again, my thoughts snagged on the fact that she was allowed to raise me, despite having tried to kill me soon after I was born. In my mind, over the years, I had made excuses for my mother, I had reshaped and remoulded and stretched the truth out until it snapped into useless shreds in my hands.

I had told myself that the attack in the bathroom was a single moment of madness. That it was due to drink or maybe prescription drugs. That deep down, she loved me. Now, I knew differently. She had already tried to kill me as a baby and perhaps, all along, she had been biding her time, waiting for another chance, until that night in the bathroom. The calculated cruelty was astonishing. The lack of care even more so. I felt like I had not been considered at all in this whole horrible mess, and yet I was the victim. The next day, bleary-eyed from a sleepless night, I somehow got through the school run and a morning at work. Then, I called my mother's sister, her nearest surviving relative, to ask her about the first conviction.

"It was Lambeth magistrates court, in London," I said. "Do you remember it?"

"I've no idea," she replied flatly, in a voice that told me she didn't want to get involved.

Instead, I went back to see Gwen and between us, we tried to research the conviction, looking at old newspaper reports and court listings from the time. But it was over 40 years ago, and though there was a record of the charge, which said I was three months old at the time of the attack, and also a record of the conviction and sentencing, there were no other details.

"Please, call the solicitor," Gwen urged me. "It's the right thing to do."

I went home feeling like I'd been riding on a rollercoaster all day. I could barely walk in a straight line.

"What's up, Mum?" Beth asked, as I slumped onto the sofa. I didn't even have the energy to take off my coat.

"Oh, nothing darling, busy day at work," I said.

My load was heavy enough. I didn't want my children to have to carry it too. For months, I tried to ignore this new discovery, as I had with everything else. I wanted to stuff it back in a box, squashed in with the physical and sexual assaults, and just forget it. If I could have had my memory wiped, like the plot of a terrible sci-fi film, I would have jumped at the chance. Yet there was no easy escape, no magic button, and night after night, Gwen's words crept stubbornly into my thoughts and my dreams.

It's the right thing to do.

In time, the CID officers contacted me again, saying that they had spoken to members of the Stewart family. Steven was deceased. Mr Stewart had denied physical abuse or cruelty.

"It's your word against theirs," the officer said. "It's such a long time ago."

I bristled.

"I'm telling the truth," I said grimly. "They know that. What about all the other children who were fostered there? Surely there are records, surely the Stewarts could tell you their names and addresses? Those children would confirm what a hellhole that place was."

The CID officer hesitated.

"I'm really sorry, Monica," she said. "We haven't been able to trace a single one of the children who was fostered by the Stewarts. The records were not very thorough back in those days and the Stewarts said they couldn't remember."

Again, it felt as though the world was turning on me, as though everyone was conspiring against me. I had been shoved around and trodden on by the Stewart family all through my childhood – and now it was happening again. Deep down, if I was honest, I had never really expected anything more.

"If any new evidence emerges, we will let you know," the officer promised.

Later, in another endless, sleepless night, I was tormented by a blizzard of memories, rushing past my face, so close, so real, I felt I could reach out and reel them in. I remembered being pushed up against the bedroom wall and prodded and groped. I had flashbacks to Steven creeping into my room and softly telling me that I was his special sister, that he loved me most of all, whilst inflicting the most horrific pain upon me. Lifelong scarring. I switched on the bedside light, soaked with sweat and shivering violently.

"No," I begged, with my head in my hands. "No, make it stop."

As the night wore on, my anger and frustration gave way to fear and anxiety. What if the Stewarts came after me? They might possibly be furious that I had made an allegation, after all these years. What if they found me, and wanted to punish me? I still lived in the same area, I wasn't difficult to track down. I began to worry, irrationally, that they might target me or my children in some way.

What goes on in this house, stays in this house.

I had broken the golden rule. I had opened my mouth. And for what? Nothing had come of my police complaint. I ought to have known that. I was foolish and naïve for thinking that the police would listen to someone like me, that they would believe me, over people like Mr Stewart. It was the same as always. I didn't matter then and I didn't matter now.

For weeks afterwards, I lived on tenterhooks, as my anxiety tipped over into paranoia. I worried every time there was a knock at the door or the phone rang. I kept an even closer eye than usual on the children. There was no basis for my worries, I hadn't even seen the Stewart family for many years. But I couldn't help my panic. Mr Stewart still controlled me, mentally, even now.

It was almost another year before I finally plucked up the courage to contact the solicitor, Paul Brown. I made an appointment to see him, and he agreed immediately to take on my case.

Over the next few months, in hour after hour of baring my soul, Paul and his assistants built up the clearest picture yet of my childhood. This was a far more in-depth and detailed account than I had given to the police. And for the first time, I actually relived the pain, the fear, the outrage, moment by moment.

"I don't blame Mrs Stewart," I told the assistant. "She was never physically abusive. And sometimes she was quite nice to me. But Mr Stewart destroyed me. The physical punishments from him were bad. But the mental abuse was worse. I felt completely worthless, and in fact, I still do."

I described my ordeal aged seven, lying in my bunkbed, with Steven standing over me. And again, the details flooded back. I was remembering more and more, as the days passed.

"It is sexual assault," the assistant reminded me. "You need to accept that."

Slowly, very slowly, I was starting to believe it.

"I know," I wept.

By the end of the final session, I was sobbing uncontrollably, and yet I felt an incredible sense of release and catharsis. It was like going through a door which had been locked all my life. I had walked past it every single day, afraid to even rattle the handle. Now I was smashing the locks, I was wrenching it from the hinges, and I was marching through. Here I am! Listen to my voice!

31

The Same Root Rule

I'd had no contact at all from my father since I was a teenager, following that night when he and Mum had argued, and she had ripped his suit jacket in a drunken rage. We hadn't even exchanged Christmas cards since and as far as I was aware, he knew nothing of me or my children. I didn't even know whether he was still alive. But one day in 2010, my sister-in-law, Liz, called me, full of excitement.

"You won't believe who's living at Hillside Crescent," she said. "I just found out today."

"Who?" I asked, mystified.

"Your dad, Mon," she replied. "Your dad lives on Hillside Crescent. It's amazing."

The coincidence was mind-blowing. I had lived there as a child, until I was taken into foster care. My grandparents, and my mother, had all lived on that same road. I had always felt an embryonic attachment to the place. And now, Dad was there too.

"Do you want to go and see him?" Liz asked. "I'll come with you."

I knew Dad must be in his early 80s by now, as he was

much older than Mum. Perhaps this was fate, giving us one last chance of a reunion.

"Let's go now," I said to Liz, already grabbing my bag and keys. "No time like the present!"

I couldn't wait. But, as we turned into Hillside Crescent, my nerves began to jangle. I hadn't seen Dad for over thirty years, after all. And just being on this road, where I'd once been so happy, especially spending time with Granny and Grandpa, was quite overwhelming. I had to blink back the tears as we began asking around the neighbours for Dad's house. It didn't take us long to find him.

"That one over there," a lady told us. "That's Charlie Mount's place."

My jaw dropped. She was pointing at a front door directly opposite Mum's old house. Opposite my old house.

"Problem is," she continued. "He was taken into a care home a few weeks ago. That's still his house, but I think it's empty now."

My heart sank. We managed to get the name of the care home from another neighbour and the next day, I turned up at visiting time.

"We already knew he had a daughter called Monica," the nurse told me. "His other children visit him. You're the only one he's been waiting for."

I smiled.

"Well, I'm here now," I said.

The nurse explained Dad was in quite good health; he was just old and infirm and needed help with his personal care.

"Charlie, here's a visitor for you," she said brightly, as we reached his bedroom.

I choked back the emotion as I took his hand in mine. He was frail and he had lost lots of weight. But he was still, undeniably, my father. Even though he was in bed, in his night clothes, there was a definite air of pride about him. He held his shoulders back, and his pyjamas were neatly pressed. He was the same, smart man I remembered, still so polished.

"I'm here, Dad," I said softly, stroking his hand, the skin as thin as parchment.

He croaked a reply and his eyes shone with happiness.

There was so much to say, and yet at the same time, the silence was enough.

"I'll be back again soon," I promised him.

But in the early hours of the next morning, I got a call from the care home.

"I'm afraid your dad took a bad turn during the night," the nurse said. "He's been taken to hospital."

I dressed quickly and woke the children. When we arrived at the ward, Dad was semi-conscious.

"Here are your grandchildren," I said, introducing my brood.

Beth stroked his head and sang to him, all the old songs which I knew he loved. Craig held his hands and Georgia sat at the end of the bed and swung her legs. Gazing at him, I felt only love, as the bitter memories of the past melted away like so many snowflakes.

"I'll be back to see him again tomorrow," I told the hospital staff. "Please call me if there's any change."

In the early hours of the next morning, my phone rang again, and, as I'd feared, it was the ward sister at the hospital.

"You need to come quickly," she said.

I pulled my clothes over my pyjamas and dashed to see Dad. But, as I arrived, a nurse gently took me aside and shook her head.

"You just missed him," she said. "He's gone."

Dad had died just three days after I'd tracked him down. I felt certain he had been hanging on to see me, to say goodbye. At his funeral, I felt a sense of peace and closure and gratitude that we'd been able to share those final precious moments.

* * * *

With the crushing news that the police did not intend to pursue a criminal conviction, I was more determined than ever to pursue my case through the civil route. I didn't care about compensation, but I did want justice. I needed justice. After years of silence and secrecy, I wanted the world to know what had happened to me as a baby, as a five-year-old, and then beyond. But Paul Brown explained to me that we were blocked from claiming through the Criminal Injuries Compensation Authority (CICA), by something called the 'same roof rule.'

"I've never even heard of it," I admitted.

Paul said that under the rule, victims of violent crimes which took place before 1979 were blocked from receiving compensation if the attacker was someone they were living with at the time of the incident. The rule came into force because of previous difficulties establishing the facts in domestic cases and also the possibility that any compensation might benefit the offender as well as the victim. "That rule applies to you," he said. "Because the abuse took place before, and also after, 1979, and with each incidence, you lived with your attackers."

"What?" I exclaimed.

I had never heard of anything so ridiculous, or so terribly and patently unfair. It made no sense.

"So, if my attacker had been a stranger, or even a neighbour, or perhaps a foster sibling who lived in a different house, then I could apply for compensation without a problem?" I asked. "I just don't get it. I am being punished because I lived with my mother, and then with my foster family. How is that reasonable?"

It felt like yet another hurdle, another brick wall, purposely constructed to make me suffer. The ruling made me feel even more unimportant, as though I, and people like me, just did not matter at all. In many ways, I felt it was so much worse to be attacked by someone from the same house, because of the issues of trust and of the complexity of the relationships involved.

"It is not fair," I said. "It really isn't."

Paul Brown agreed that the rule was unjust and well overdue for challenge.

"If you like, we could take on the courts and try to overturn the ruling. It's a huge task, but if we succeed, it means other victims can apply too. Have a think about it."

But I was already nodding.

"I've spent years delaying this," I said. "Let's go for it."

One Saturday, the following summer, I went into town to

do some errands. I was wandering quite aimlessly down the high street when, in the distance, my eyes settled with pin-ball precision on a figure coming towards me. He had white hair and a white beard and a stocky build. A little like Santa. Yet nothing like Santa. It was him. It was undeniably him.

"No!" I gasped out loud.

I stood, frozen, screwed to the spot, as he drew nearer and nearer. Across my eyeline, I had a violent, paralysing, flashback. I heard the back door slamming shut. I heard his footsteps on the stairs. I even heard my voice quavering as I counted: 'Five, six, seven…'

There I was, slapped over his knee, with my nightie pulled up. I could taste the blood as I bit down on my lip to quieten my screams. And then, before I knew it, I was running. Running like my life depended on it. Errands forgotten, trip abandoned, I ran all the way back home.

"What's happened?" Beth asked. "Mum, you look so pale. What is it?"

"I'm OK," I stuttered. "I'm alright. Just a funny turn, that's all."

I knew, if I'd stayed to confront Mr Stewart, he would maybe have crumbled and dissolved like any other bully. But even though I was a grown woman with my own family, my own home and a job, he still terrified me. I was too scared to face him. Too scared to even share the same street as him. Even now, he had an authority over me, a vice-like hold, that was as powerful as it was irrational.

Thick as two short planks Monica, that's you…

Pushing the scene to the back of my mind, I vowed not to

let it affect me. I had, after all, gone about my daily life for nearly 30 years without bumping into any of the Stewarts in public. I reassured myself that it was a coincidence, a freak occurrence, and nothing more.

But just weeks later, I was shopping in Morrisons one afternoon when, through the full-length windows, I caught sight of Mr Stewart once again. In that moment I had a thousand simultaneous memories; him saying grace at the table, as I bowed my head, aged five. Him lining me up, aged seven, in the hallway, threatening me with the lie detector test. Him laughing at me, aged sixteen, when I failed my school exams.

You'll never amount to anything…

He was clearly leaving the store, carrying a shopping bag, whilst I was still inside. I shrank back behind a tower of tinned fruit, my mind suddenly whirring and whizzing, my shopping list forgotten.

I just wanted to run away, yet I could not risk bumping into him outside in the car park. Fishing my phone out of my handbag, I dialled my friend, Michelle.

"He's outside! Mr Stewart is outside the shop!" I whispered. "What if he sees me, Michelle? What shall I do?"

I didn't even dare say it out loud in case he somehow heard me through the wall.

"Don't worry," she soothed. "It's fine. Just stay in the shop. Go and get a coffee, there's a café at the back of the supermarket, isn't there? By the time you're finished, he will have gone.

"He can't hurt you now, Mon. Remember that."

I followed Michelle's instructions, and, as I sat in the café, I repeated her words over and over to myself.

He can't hurt you now...

But that second sighting, so soon after the first, was unsettling. And afterwards, I changed my shopping habits and my daily routine completely. For months, I went to a different supermarket on different days and at different times. I could not risk seeing him again. I could not explain it; I knew he could no longer get to me and yet the fear was as strong and as potent as it ever had been.

In years to come, I would hear that Mr Stewart had passed away. He was remembered very kindly. My blood curdled as I thought of the man I knew. And even then, knowing he was dead, I felt no relief, no comfort. The dread was still there, in the pit of my stomach. I could not escape him. Even death could not save me.

"I won't ever be truly free of him," I admitted to Michelle. "Ever."

My legal challenge, meanwhile, demanding changes to the Criminal Injuries Compensation scheme, was moving very slowly.

We had initially applied directly to CICA for compensation and though we expected the rejection, the letter, when it came, was still a blow.

We then requested a review of the decision which was, again, refused.

The decision made by the review panel said: "We have looked carefully at the reasons for review, and I am sorry that I cannot make a full or reduced award because under the scheme, we cannot pay compensation if your client was a victim of a crime of violence before October 1 1979 and was living with the assailant at the time as members of the same family. We have no discretion in this.

"I am sorry to give what I am certain will be disappointing news."

On my behalf, Paul Brown had argued that my human rights were being breached because I was deprived of support under the rule that dismissed entitlement to compensation for injuries caused by someone within the same family. We challenged the rule on the basis of discrimination and a violation of my human rights.

"We won't give up," he told me. "There's still a long way to go."

Next, our case was heard before a first-tier tribunal and a panel made up of judges. I was required to give evidence and it was nerve-racking. Afterwards, the tribunal found that I was a 'reliable and credible witness' and 'consistent in (her) story.'

But though my account of the abuse was accepted and believed, our application to overturn the same roof rule was refused.

It was so frustrating. And for me, the more I read and heard about this rule, the more determined I became to overturn it, not just for my sake, but for the hundreds of other people who were also affected by it.

Our case was then heard in 2016 at the Outer House of the Scottish Court of Session. Again, we won most of the argument, but not all. It still, infuriatingly, was not enough.

Judges at the Court of Session accepted that my human rights had been breached, but said the government was entitled for policy reasons not to backdate changes made to the scheme in 1979 which scrapped the so-called 'same roof' rule.

Lord Burns admitted that the rule was discriminatory but said that the government were "entitled to take a cautious approach and to impose a cut-off date to mitigate the effects of change".

Lord Burns recognised the 'same roof' rule was changed after it appeared to CICA that the exclusion of children who were assaulted by their parents appeared to be unjustified.

"The rule does impose a 'bright line' rule which excludes claims for injuries occurring before the relevant date. It thus does discriminate. But it was done in that way because it was not thought possible to estimate the cost of abolition," said Lord Burns.

He added: "The petitioner is a victim of violent crime perpetrated when she was a child. Because she was assaulted by her mother in the family home, she is denied compensation under the same roof rule.

"If her mother had assaulted a friend of the complainer's, at the same time, that child would be entitled to advance a claim. Both would be child victims of violent crime. That is enough in my view to demonstrate a difference in treatment between persons in 'analogous situations'."

One of the key problems surrounded the long-term sustainability of the scheme, if it was hit by retrospective claims from victims from before 1979, of which I, of course, was one.

I failed to win a judicial review to the Inner House of the Court of Session which held that it was within the government's discretion not to backdate a change to the scheme.

The second most senior judge in Scotland, Lady Dorrian, the Lord Justice Clerk, in delivering the judgement said: "The restriction of the scheme was a prudent policy decision concerning the allocation of finite resources in a matter of socio-economic policy."

Yet still, I refused to give up. Eventually, we were successful in securing a date to attend the Inner House of the Court of Session – the highest civil court in Scotland. I had decided to attend, and Beth offered to come with me, both of us catching the early 7am bus to Edinburgh.

On the morning of the case, I was up by 5.30am, and got dressed into a smart pair of grey trousers, a cream blouse and my best high heels. Beth wore a lovely dress and heels.

"We could be off to a party," she joked.

I tried to smile but my mouth was dry with nerves. I wanted us to make a good impression and yet at the same time, I knew that it shouldn't matter at all if my make-up was smudged or whether my hair was blow-dried. This was about justice. I felt such a weight of responsibility, not simply for myself but for everyone else, who like me, had been abused and denied their rights under the same roof rule. I badly wanted to change the system and all its flaws. But carrying the burden for everyone was huge.

"You'll be OK," Beth promised me. "Whatever happens Mum, you should be proud. You've come a long way."

By 6.50am, in the murky winter drizzle, we were ready

and waiting at the bus stop, huddled under an umbrella. The bus trundled all the way into the centre of Edinburgh, and the courthouse, sitting near to Edinburgh Castle, looked as intimidating as it was impressive.

"Wow," I whistled. "Well, here we are."

Outside we met with Paul Brown and another solicitor, Kirsti Nelson. I was also introduced to a QC and another legal official. To me, it was a whirlwind of grand black cloaks and fancy vocabulary. To say that I felt out of my depth was an understatement and I was so glad I had Beth beside me to squeeze my hand and roll her eyes conspiratorially when she knew nobody was looking.

"This way, please," said an usher, and we were directed down a long hallway towards a small meeting room. All along the hallway there were barristers rushing up and down, having heated discussions either on the phone or with clients who jogged alongside them.

"Why can't they just stand still and chat?" I asked, perplexed.

"Oh, that's so that nobody can listen in to their conversations," my solicitor told me with a smile.

On the hallway walls were old-fashioned paintings of legal bigwigs from years gone by. It was fascinating, a little like a walking history lesson. We spent some time in the meeting room before my name was called. All at once, I felt my stomach plunging.

"Don't worry," Kirsti reassured me. "The QC will do all the talking. You just have to listen."

And it was just as well. Because when the QC began

his opening speech, I at first wondered if he was speaking a foreign language. I couldn't make any sense of the legal arguments at all. There were three judges who listened to each baffling argument in turn and made even more baffling comments back.

Beth and I had made such an early start that morning, and I was exhausted. In the warmth of the courtroom, I felt myself dozing off.

"Mum!" Beth hissed. "You were starting to snore there!"

At lunchtime, we followed everyone else downstairs to the most stunning restaurant I had ever seen. There were beautiful round glass tables dotted around the room and the chairs were upholstered in rich and vibrant colours of velvet. The waiters glided past us, trays held high, with white cloths draped over their forearms.

"Gosh," Beth whistled. "This place is something else."

I sank into one of the fabulous chairs and felt that I never wanted to leave. I was so comfortable. But then, I caught sight of the menu – and the prices.

"No way we're eating here," I said, sitting up abruptly. "Let's just have a lemonade and then we'll get a sausage roll each from Greggs!"

The afternoon session was much the same as the morning, boring in some ways but also fascinating. I felt so privileged even to be there and to have got this far. After the session ended, Beth and I had a quick look around the shops, limping by now in our high heels, before queuing for the bus back home.

"I'm glad we don't do that every day," Beth said, kicking

off her shoes and rubbing her soles as we sat down on the bus.

"We couldn't afford to!" I laughed. "Remember those prices in the restaurant! I'd need a bank loan to have my dinner in there."

It was an eye-opener, that was for sure. I could only hope that those puzzling courtroom arguments would, eventually, be translated into victory for me.

32

Seeking Justice

Sadly, we won most, but not all, of the argument to the Inner House. It was disappointing, and to me, it seemed dreadfully unreasonable. But Paul Brown vowed not to give up and instead took the appeal to the highest court in the country, the Supreme Court. This was to be our final chance.

The story of my case hit the local and national press and a spokesman for the Ministry of Justice commented: "We deeply sympathise with anyone who has been the victim of violent crime.

"The Criminal Injuries Compensation Scheme did not previously allow payments to be awarded when the offender and victim lived in the same house as members of the same family."

We learned there was a similar case in England, and one in Northern Ireland, and the decision of the Supreme Court would therefore affect us all as one, and of course the many other silent victims of abuse around the UK.

I could only cross my fingers and hope. I was so used to being let down, forgotten and pushed aside, that in truth I held out very little faith at all.

And, as we waited for what would be our final attempt at justice, our lives continued as normal. As always, I concentrated on my family and, as they got older and more independent, I focussed more on my career too.

I studied administration at college and later worked in a homeless unit for 16-21 year olds. I could relate well to the lost souls who came through our doors and sometimes I was more of a surrogate mother or a counsellor than a support worker. I had a job in a dementia unit too. I knew how damaging it was to grow up without love or care. Yet despite this, or perhaps because of it, I had worked my entire adult life in the care industry, either in hospitals, care homes or specialist units.

After leaving school, Audrey studied childcare. Craig continued to bravely battle his problems and the girls were always so supportive of him. He made great progress and I was really proud of the young man he had become. I was thankful that my children shared a special bond, and I was equally proud of them all, in different ways.

Beth worked in a care home, looking after the elderly, after she finished her education. Though she had always been confident, she was pretty quiet, and her job helped to really bring her out of her shell. It was lovely to see. She had a great group of friends and a busy social life. In 2016, she had a baby boy, Alfie, and five years later, she gave birth to a little girl, Esme. I adored my grandchildren, each one a blessing, each one a reason to look to the future with hope. When Alfie was learning to talk, he called me 'Gaga' and the name has stuck to this day.

Georgia was, like Beth, a quiet girl but very level-headed and reliable and with a fantastic group of pals. At primary school, Georgia announced that she wanted to learn to play the saxophone and I saved hard for her lessons and tried not to wince as she practised her scales loudly each night. I loved that she was trying something new, even if it did drown out the TV. But the comparisons with my own childhood were impossible to hide away from; I thought often of the piano, ostentatiously placed in the hallway at the Stewart house, a symbol of respectability and grandeur, but out of bounds for a foster child like myself.

Towards the end of high school, Georgia got a part-time job and planned to study beauty at college. She was the only one left at home and I'd bought her a little puppy called Bear, half Poodle and half Chihuahua, and he was our baby. We spoiled him rotten.

And Melanie was very much a part of our lives. One Christmas, Beth bought me the most beautiful gift and when I unwrapped it, I burst into a flood of emotional tears. It was a decoration for the tree, made of two feathered angel wings with the name Melanie in the centre. It became our most treasured Christmas ornament, a reminder that Melanie was with us always.

* * * *

In February 2019, our case was due to be heard at the Supreme Court, alongside the cases in London and Northern Ireland. Though there were two other applicants, as well as myself, I didn't know who they were.

One morning, days before the hearing, my phone rang. I recognised Paul Brown's number, and, with shaking hands, I swiped to take the call.

"You did it, Monica!" he announced. "The government has withdrawn their opposition. They threw in the towel. We can submit your claim."

I was thrilled; totally dumbfounded. As the emotions rushed through me, I found I could barely speak.

"Thank you, thank you," I stuttered. "I need to ring the kids. I need to let them know."

As I called my children with the news, they all whooped and screamed in celebration.

"Proud of you, Mum," Beth yelled. "You did it!"

I sent Georgia a quick text message at school and then my phone rang again. This time it was the *BBC*. Then it was *The Daily Record*. Then a radio station. All wanting an interview – with me!

I had discussed the issue of waiving my anonymity with Paul Brown previously and for me, there was no doubt. I absolutely wanted to have my name and face in the media, because it was the only way that other victims of abuse would read about the change of rule, and realise that they, too, could come forward.

"It's not as if CICA are going to write to all these people and say: 'Hey! Send us your application!'" I said grimly. "The only way we can make this public is if I speak out. And I'll shout it from the rooftops, no problem.

"I've kept quiet for far too long."

I did a raft of interviews that same day, and whilst it was

tiring, it was extremely liberating. I was riding high. "You're a celebrity now," Georgia giggled, as she arrived home. "I'll have to get a limo to school tomorrow!"

Late in the evening, I got together with the kids, and we shared a bottle of bubbly.

"Thank you," I smiled. "Thank you, to you all. Your love keeps me strong. This victory belongs to all of us."

In bed that night, I focused not on my mother or on the Stewart family. My thoughts instead drifted to the hundreds, even thousands, of people who might benefit from the new rule change. As I knew only too well, abuse victims often carried the secret for decades before they felt able to speak out. After all, it had taken me fifty years from that first assault, as a baby, to find my voice. Fifty years of secrets and suffering. Some of those people, like me, would have claims dating back before 1979. Now, thanks to the court victory, and the coverage in the media, they would see justice done. Their voices would be heard.

That week, the press attention was crazy. I did TV and radio interviews and there were articles in newspapers right across the UK. The two other applicants, from London and Northern Ireland, remained anonymous. And whilst I understood their need for privacy, I knew that I was doing the right thing by sharing my story. I had, after all, stayed silent for most of my life.

Later that month, I got a message from the *Glasgow Times* to say I'd been nominated for the annual Scotswoman of the Year Award 2018.

"Me?" I asked, incredulously. "Are you sure?"

I couldn't believe it. It was a huge shock, but an honour too. From 300 nominees I made it to the final shortlist of just five women. In March 2019, I attended a glitzy ball at the Principal Grand Central Hotel in Glasgow where, though I didn't win the final prize, I had the time of my life. And in the taxi home, in my beautiful dress with my sequined bag and my towering heels, I really felt as though I was seeing stars. And it had nothing to do with the champagne.

You'll never amount to anything, Monica... Thick as two short planks...

"Well, you were wrong there," I said to myself with a little smile. "I have four wonderful kids, I have a job, I have a nice home and I'm a finalist for Scotswoman of the Year. Not bad eh, for a hopeless case?"

* * * *

Gradually, the press interest died away and our lives returned to normal. Paul Brown submitted my application for compensation, in relation to both the sexual abuse in foster care and the two attacks by my mother. I was assessed by a psychiatrist, which felt at once like an unburdening and an over-facing. The report concluded that:

'Her sense of self is weak and unstable...there are chronic feelings of emptiness.'

I was diagnosed with Emotionally Unstable Personality Disorder and Post Traumatic Stress Disorder, with long term health problems such as headaches, persistent low mood, chronic bloating and sickness, reflux and vomiting, dizzy spells, palpitations, tiredness, anxiety and depression.

The psychiatrist found that my regular bouts of sickness, and my ongoing dental problems, all dated back to the malnutrition I'd suffered as a child, and by the brutal punishments I received for not eating my meals.

It was explained to me that the physical abuse from Mr Stewart would be recorded but that I would not be awarded compensation in respect of this, as CICA would focus on the more serious offence of the sexual abuse. I was warned, as always, there would be quite a wait. In the meantime, I tried to thrust the whole business to one side.

Yet now that my memories were out in the open, and my story was out in the public eye, I could not simply repackage it and freeze it, as I had done so effectively in the past. My mind buzzed constantly with snapshots from my childhood; the horrible black shoes, the speckled brown carpet, the tartan skirt I wore for church. I recalled my mother's glassy eyes, her lacquered hair, her flared jeans. They were broken recollections, falling out in no particular order and making no particular sense. I remembered my mother screaming when my father pushed her hand through the window. I remembered her laughing as I held down the nozzle on the hair spray.

Just say, 'Stop' Mummy!

As time went on, I began to feel harassed and harangued as if my past would not leave me alone, as if it was prodding and poking me and trying to ruin me. I couldn't sleep and I couldn't concentrate. I felt tormented to the point that I was breaking.

This disintegration didn't make sense to me. I had done the

hard part; I had spoken out, I had shared my secrets, I had taken on the government, and I had won. I had every reason to feel proud and victorious. And at times, I did feel briefly euphoric. I was on top of the world. But these moments were followed by crushing lows and a despair so deep and paralysing that I could barely get out of bed. Wave after wave crashed over me, of happiness or sadness, I couldn't even tell. Possibly it was a mixture of both.

My childhood memories were like a virus, dormant for so many years but emerging now, stronger and more virulent, ready to paralyse my entire body with their toxicity. I struggled through each day, barely keeping the flashbacks at bay. And at night, I had horrific 3D nightmares which left me hot and cold, sweating and shivering, and scared. So scared.

I had always, throughout my adult life, had a fear that I would die young. It is a worry that many single mothers must surely endure; the concern over how our children would cope if something happened to us. Above all, I wanted security and safety and a loving environment for my children. I could not bear the idea of them struggling on, without me. That fear of a premature death grew and grew, like a malignancy, until it was blocking my vision. I was generally quite healthy so there was no basis to my belief, but it stemmed, in part at least, from my mother making two attempts on my life. Even though she was dead, I started to worry that perhaps she might orchestrate a third attempt, from beyond the grave. I began to panic, without reason, that she would get me, in the end.

I couldn't bear to be in an empty house or even in a quiet house and I became convinced that something very bad was about to happen to me. I constantly checked the windows and doors. I had to have all the internal doors open, and I had to have noise and movement; signs of life within the home.

My sleep was disturbed and splintered, and I had horrible nightmares where the faces of my tormentors danced malevolently before me; my mother, Steven, Mr Stewart himself. Many of my dreams centred around water and drowning and I'd wake, gasping and choking and screaming in fear of my life.

"No!" I pleaded. "Please let me go!"

I began making excuses not to leave the house, believing that it was safer for me to remain indoors. Georgia was old enough to go to and from school on her own and so I saw my GP and was signed off work with depression and anxiety. So now, there was no reason at all for me to go outside. Instead, I spent my days curled up in bed, in a foetal position, underneath a blanket. I was all too aware of the echoes from my own childhood, and with a horrifying jolt, I realised that this was almost exactly how my mother had spent her days too.

I even had the TV on constantly, craving background noise and distraction, just as she once had. Was I turning into her? Or was this a desperate attempt to rewind, to revisit my childhood and start again? I had no idea. But the link with my mother was terrifying. It was immobilising.

"I will not be like her," I vowed. "I will not let this ruin me."

I kept a bottle of Lucozade at the side of my bed, as a nod to my dear old Granny. It had been her favourite drink, and this was my way of keeping her close. During those dark months, Beth became my guardian angel; she cared for me, and she looked out for Craig and Georgia too.

"I'm here for you, Mum," she told me. "Just as you've always been here for us."

But as 2021 rolled around, I made a decision. I'd spent almost two years in a thick, deep depression. For my sake, and for my children's sake, I had to drag myself out of it. Each day, I felt as though I made maybe a millimetre of progress. But I kept on going. I kept on pushing myself forwards. I forced myself to leave the bedroom, and to go downstairs, just to have a glass of juice and a chat with Georgia. With Beth's support, I was soon strong enough to leave the house, to see friends, to gradually join the world once again. I even made plans to redecorate the bedrooms, starting with Georgia's first of all.

"Mum, you can do this," she beamed. "I know you can."

It was just me and her in the family home now, along with her dog, Bear. I owed it to her to get well again. Once again, my children were my crutch and I leaned on them more than ever before.

Epilogue

Mid-way through 2022, I feel as though I'm battling my anxiety and I'm moving forwards. But some scars will never fade; at least, not completely. I have a lovely bathroom with a jacuzzi bath, and LED colour-change lights which control the colour of the bath water. I even have a surround sound system. It's the perfect setting for a long soak. The kids love my fancy bath, Craig especially, and of course my little grandchildren do too. And yet, I've never put so much as a toe in the water myself – I always take a shower! My friends laugh gently at my water phobia, and I've learned to laugh about it too.

"Take a bath yourself if you like it so much," I tell them. "Personally, I feel it's overrated!"

I still can't have the internal doors in my home fully closed. I am unsure whether this relates to the attack by my mother, when she tried to drown me. The bathroom door was closed tight on that occasion, and that trauma haunts me still. Or perhaps it's a more general neurosis; I grew up with closed doors and tight lips. I was raised with silence and with secrets. Now, in my own home, I insist on open doors and open minds. It drives Georgia mad when she has her friends around; sometimes they'd just like a little privacy to gossip, and she wants to close her bedroom door.

"No," I tell her. "Just leave an inch gap. I can't let you close it."

In return, I agree to stay downstairs so that she knows I'm not eavesdropping. Between us, we find a way.

My cleaning obsession, which began as a child when I was made to forensically clean my bedroom at the Stewarts' house, has lasted right through my adult life. I am always polishing, scrubbing, and hoovering. I can't bear to see a speck of fluff on the carpet or a line of dust along the skirting board. My OCD gives me certainty in a world where I have often floundered in chaos.

Because of my alcohol problems as a teenager, I drink very rarely, and never more than a single glass of wine. I don't like taking medication because I saw what it did to my mother. Even now, when I'm nervous, I vomit. If I'm faced with a big meal, I feel my stomach churning. That fear, though it's pushed right down inside me, will never fully dissolve. I'm carrying a lot of baggage. And yet, it gets lighter with every day.

I have recently received compensation from CICA in relation to the sexual abuse I suffered in foster care. I have not yet settled on an agreement for compensation with regards to the attacks from my mother. That application is still ongoing and should be resolved this year.

Strangely enough, though I felt like an outsider as a child,

I've kept the same group of school friends all through my teenage years and into my adult life. I've remained resolutely single since splitting from Georgia's dad and so I rely on my friends.

Michelle, my best friend from high school, is my best pal even now. It's ironic that I have at times felt so alone and lonely, and yet I have the most wonderful friends around me. We go away on holidays or on nights out together and we love to reminisce. We laugh about the hungry cow 'eating' my shoes. And we giggle about me stealing the collection money in church for a penny chew. We don't laugh so much about the suitcase for my sixteenth birthday. I won't ever see the humour in that particular occasion. Certainly, we never laugh about the abuse, the cruelty, the suffering.

"We knew the Stewarts were odd, but we had no idea what you were going through," Michelle told me. "I wish we could have supported you more. I wish we'd known."

"I hardly knew what was happening myself," I reassured her. "It was my way of coping. I blotted it out. You did what you could. You were there for me, and you still are."

I can never thank my friends enough. But most of all, I would like to thank my children.

Having my babies was the making of me as a person and I believe I've survived and flourished because of them. Only with their support and love did I feel strong enough to take on the government and change the rules, not just for me, but for so many other victims of abuse. I feel as though it's the perfect positive antidote to all the suffering from my childhood.

And perhaps my final word should go to my dear Granny; long-gone now, but she lives on in my heart and her kind words are a comfort to me still:

Never forget you are loved, Monica. Never.

Less than two years after the government's abolition of the 'same roof' rule, it was estimated that more than £20 million was offered to thousands of victims who applied for compensation.

Acknowledgements

Thank you to Michelle Moore, my lifelong friend,
to Liz Bruce and Susan Kennedy. Thank you for
always standing by my side.

And to anyone who has suffered at the hands of others,
use the strength and courage that has taken you this far to
make YOUR own ending, take your control back because
YOU MATTER!

And finally to Ann Cusack for her understanding, patience
and brilliance through doing this book, thank you.

Monica Allan, 2023.

Other bestselling Mirror Books

The Asylum
Carol Minto

With Ann and Joe Cusack

Born into poverty and with mostly absent parents, Carol helped to raise her nine siblings. But when she was just 11 years old, her older brother began to sexually abuse her.

After four years, Carol managed to escape – and ran away from home. Picked up by social services they placed her at the infamous Aston Hall psychiatric hospital in Derby where she was stripped, sedated, assaulted and raped by the doctor in charge.

This is the full story of how she overcame unimaginable suffering, to find the solace she has today as a mother and grandmother.

MIRROR BOOKS

written by Ann and Joe Cusack

The Boy With
A Pound In His Pocket

Jade Akoum

With Ann and Joe Cusack

**Yousef Makki was stabbed in the heart by one
of his friends on a quiet, leafy street in the wealthy
Manchester suburb of Hale Barns.**

Just four months after he was killed, a jury found his friend not
guilty of murder or manslaughter. Yousef died from a single stab
wound to the chest.

When his sister, Jade, collected his blood-stained clothes, he had
a single pound coin in his pocket. This is Jade's moving, personal
story of how the fight for justice has transformed her life.

MIRROR BOOKS

A Mother's Job
Joy Dove

With Ann and Joe Cusack

While Jodey Whiting was stuck in hospital battling pneumonia over Christmas, a letter dropped on her doormat from the Department for Work and Pensions, asking her to attend an assessment. It was a letter she never saw...

Despite suffering from major health problems and needing daily care, the powers-that-be callously halted benefit payments for the mum-of-nine. While waiting for her appeal, and with no money coming in, Jodey killed herself, aged just 42. This is the story of her mother Joy's brave and inspirational fight for justice.

MIRROR BOOKS